GW00360048

TIl

TRAVEL

Through Consciousness and
Advanced Technology

FREDERICK DODSON

COPYRIGHT

The Copyright of this work lies with the author. Any unauthorized reproduction without the authors written consent, will be handled legally.

Copyright © 2020 Frederick Dodson
All rights reserved.
ISBN: 9781661790868

DISCLAIMER

The author is not responsible for effects readers have or allegedly have from this book, just like a driving school instructor is not responsible for his students driving. Furthermore, the information provided in this book is not a substitute for conventional medical assistance.

Table of Contents

This books intention was to write something beautiful that didn't exist yet.

1

Methods of Time Travel

The experience of the "paranormal" is a *personal choice*. Time Travel is a personal choice. Hard proof of these events is hard to come by because they are meant to be personal, open only to those ready to receive. Proof of the paranormal is easy to come by, if you keep it personal, with no need to prove anything. Life is set up, so a human being perceives what they can handle, asked for and deserve. That's why many will have a supernatural experience when alone, but fail in front of a live audience. Shared paranormal experiences do exist, but they are rare.

Supernatural events, such as Time Travel, usually feel natural while they are being experienced, but when later reported, are exaggerated to sound bigger than they were. Instead of lessons, the stories become entertainment vehicles of the Ego. And though time travel is amazing and beautiful, I don't think it's as far-out as commonly believed. It can be used for exploration of the Multi-verse, by anyone. It only seems "far out crazy" to those tricked into believing in linear, fixed time. Almost every news article I read on the topic, while researching for this book, referred to it as "whacky", "crazy", "far out" and "mind boggling. How small minded would you have to be to see it that way?

Did you know that clocks or watches in Satellites above the earth are tuned to run slower than clocks on Earth?

That's because time runs quicker outside of Earth. We live in denser gravity on the surface of Earth. A slowing of time is linked to gravity and gravity comes from the density of physical masses. Less physical mass equals less gravity equals a quickening of time. This is called *time dilation*. It's why the ancient religions speak of time running differently for Beings of *Higher Realms*. Buddhist texts speak of a different time for every level and realm of consciousness. They say that at one level of consciousness, 100 Million years might pass, but for the next higher level, it's only one thousand years and for another level higher, that same span is experienced as 100 years, and so forth. I write about this in detail in my book "Journeys in Spectral Consciousness.

Or consider these Bible quotes:

"But do not forget this one thing, beloved, that one day is with the Lord as a thousand years, and a thousand years as one day." 2 Peter 3:8.

"For a thousand years in God's sight are but as yesterday when it is past, or as a watch in the night,". Psalm 90:4.

But even just going to Earth's Orbit nearby, we are subject to a different time than surface dwellers. From their perspective, we are time travelers into the future, even if only by a few seconds.

I wrote my first article on Time Travel when I was 19 years old. Looking back, I'm amused I would feel entitled to do so at such an early age. I sold it to a well-known magazine. It was 1993 and the Internet was just starting, but had not yet replaced print. 10 years later, at age 29, I published a book called "Time Travel ". As I was living in Germany at the time, I had written it in German. It is still available on Amazon, titled „Zeitreisen" by Frederick Dodson, if you care to look it up. It is now 2020. Twenty-seven years have passed since the first article and seventeen years have passed since the first book. If you've read the original book from 2003, you will find that I have borrowed some parts of that book for this one. But there are also large parts of it which I haven't borrowed, because they've become dated. It's amazing just how much information becomes outdated in only 17 years. Large parts of this book are therefore freshly written and researched.

My intention is to give you the sense that something fantastic, can sound rational and be accessible to you personally.

Maybe you are thinking about skipping chapters to read only what interests you. But this book should be taken as a whole. I talk about the intellectual, physical, technological and spiritual aspects of time travel. Grasped from all angles, it is easier to experience.

These are the commonly known methods of Time Travel:

De-Materialization

This method de-materializes the physical body into energy particles to re-materialize it at another place or time. It was popularized in the TV Series Star Trek, where it was used to teleport from the Spaceship to the surface of Planets by typing in the coordinates of the destination. It was also featured in the TV Series "Stargate". At a younger age I watched these shows with wide eyed wonderment, but today I simply think "Sure, why not?". If everything is indeed energy, then physical objects can be converted into a less dense form to be reassembled elsewhere.

There is no shortage of ancient or modern legend in which a person enters a gate, door or mirror only to appear in another space-time. Considering the vast distances of this intelligently designed Universe, it would make sense that there are shortcuts and speedways in between stars and galaxies.

Time Machines

There have been many claims of time travel devices. We'll be looking into these claims later in the book. Contemporary Physics tells us time travel is "theoretically" possible, but the cost of building the machines and the energy required to run them, is beyond what we can currently handle. They say "If we could afford it, then we could time travel". There are several prominent physicists who make this statement, if you care to look it up.

In my view, technology is not needed to accomplish something, that Consciousness can do more effectively, cost efficiently and cleanly. On the other hand, some say that time travel devices are linked to Consciousness and don't operate without it. That suggestion would seem accurate to me. At least more accurate than the idea that a time machine can exist separately from the individual using it.

Dreaming

Your own dreamscape offers time travel opportunities more accessible than multi-billion-dollar time travel devices. We have *precognitive dreams* that can take us into the future and *retro-cognitive dreams* that take us into the past. The downside is, such dreams are not easy to control, often happening randomly. Fortunately, noticing pre-cognitive dreams can be learned in only a few days, just through awareness that they exist and are surprisingly common. This type of dream proves time is neither linear nor fixed, even if the mind prefers to see it that way.

Dreamscapes exist in a more fluid time continuum. For most people, dreams in which they know they are dreaming (lucid dreams), are the first step to experiences of travel to other worlds and times. But sometimes the Lucid Dream Journey can become so fascinating that one gets sidetracked from the original intention to time travel.

Remote Viewing

This is the method I will present in this book. Instead of viewing only across space, we'll also be viewing across time. The ability itself is moderately easy to experience, but deciphering one's perceptions can take more time to learn. The problem is that remotely viewed data first needs to be differentiated from Imagination. The second issue is that some of it is symbolic and needs to be correctly interpreted.

We will use a variation of remote viewing which I have developed, to make time travel easier, more real and more enjoyable for anyone. I will also record guided audio versions of these processes and put them on my website. Don't skip forward to these methods. They work best on a mind properly prepared.

2

Pre-Cognitive Dreaming

"Space and Time are Modes of Consciousness, not attributes of the physical Universe,"- Immanuel Kant

Pre-Cognitive dreams provide a good entry point to the topic, because everyone has had them, knowingly or unknowingly, anyone can produce them consciously and they are definite *proof* of time travel.

Have you ever had a dream that is moving toward an event in the "real" waking world, such as a noise or sound and then you later wondered how your dream "knew" what would happen?

As a young teenager I once dreamed I was escaping a monster while running toward a cliff. The chase took some time, weaving through woods, rocks and fields. Finally arriving at the edge of the cliff, I had the choice to either jump or be caught by the monster. I looked back and saw the monster quickly approaching. I looked forward and saw the fall. Tough choice. I jumped. The falling took a long time, as if in slow motion. I hit the ground with a painful thud and instantly awoke. Then I realized what had been so painful: The book shelf, that me and my Dad had just built above my bed the day before, had broken and fallen on me at the very same time I hit the ground in my dream. Some books were still falling off my body onto the floor while I was waking up. The books falling on my chest and stomach caused the dream of hitting the ground. But how was it possible that my dream was leading to this event? How did the dream "know" that the bookshelf and books would later tumble down on me?

Dream Consciousness does not take place in the same *time* as Waking Life. I have had so many time anomalies, time stretches and cracks in time during dreams, that I have no doubt the "rules" of time can be bent while we sleep.

I recall a similar dream: I was walking toward a building of which I knew that it would be noisy inside. I walked toward it for a while, with mixed feelings. I didn't want to go there because I didn't like the noise. But I had Business there. When I finally opened the door, a screeching noise tore through my consciousness and I woke up. There was construction work across from my place. My window was open and one of the workers had started drilling into the street. That's the noise that had awoken me. Same question: How did my dream know that I was moving toward a noise-event? Was dream-time stretched in a way that the 1 second in which drilling started, seemed like several minutes of walking toward the event? Or was my consciousness creating a cause for something it already knew would happen? Whatever the explanation, these dreams proved to me, beyond the shadow of a doubt, that time is neither fixed nor linear.

But there is an even more common type of Precognitive dream: Those showing events that happen not while waking up, but days or even weeks later.

The first groundbreaking book on Precognitive Dreaming was written in 1927 by the aircraft engineer and mathematician J.W. Dunne, who was also involved in the construction of the first British military airplanes. His book "An Experiment in Time" created a foundation for the exploration of precognitive dreams. The book is a classic and milestone in consciousness research.

As a result of countless experiences, Dunne asked himself whether his dreams are astral travels (out of body), clairvoyance (remote viewing) or indeed telepathy with people who are having the experience at the moment he is dreaming them. After a lifetime of research, he came to the conclusion that neither of these explanations are adequate.

His discovery: Precognitive dreams are time travel to the Future. They were of things he himself would *perceive* in the future, not necessarily of what was actually happening.

An example: He had a vivid dream about the explosion of a Volcano on the Island of Mauritius, in which 4000 people died. On the next day, he read about the event in the newspaper. But he misread. As he later discovered, 40 000 had died, not 4000. His "dream journal" entry matched what he had misread, rather than the event as it really happened.

J.W. Dunne discovered that precognitive dreams were "memories of the future", events that would happen to him. Of course, he didn't only have precognitive dreams, but the more he researched and focused on them, the more common they became.

Image: J.W. Dunne, Time-Anomaly-Researcher

During an early phase of his research, Dunne once dreamed his clock showed 8:02. He woke up later and discovered it really was 8:02. That initially got him worried about "Paramnesia", which is supposedly an illness of false memory. If it were true that he had that illness then both the dream and the event in "waking" life would be dreams, or worse, false memories. His scientific attitude led him to consider every possibility, even that of being insane. He also considered possibilities such as seeing the clock through closed eyelids. That's to say he did not arrive at his later conclusion, the reality of time travel, lightly

He had his first experience in 1899 in a Hotel in Sussex, England. There he dreamed one night, that he was arguing with a waiter about what time it was. While he insisted it was 4:30 in the afternoon, the waiter maintained that it was 4:30 a.m. In the strange illogic of dream-states, Dunne concluded that his pocket watch must have stopped. In his dream, he took the watch out of his vest and found his suspicion confirmed. With the idea that his watch must have stopped, he awoke. He turned on his light to look at the clock, but to his surprise it was not beside the bed, as usual. He got up and found the clock on a cupboard. The clock really had stopped and showed 4:40. The explanation seemed to be that the clock must have stopped the previous afternoon. Dunne writes: "I must have noticed that, then forgotten it, and then again remembered it in my dream. Satisfied with that explanation, I rewound the clock. As I did not know the exact time, I kept the hands of the clock where they were".

When he woke up the next morning, another surprise awaited him. He wanted to adjust the clocks time. If it had stopped the previous afternoon and he rewound it at an unknown time at night, it must be off be several hours. But he found that it was only off by a few minutes. That was exactly the time that had passed between waking up and rewinding the clock. Which of course indicated that he dreamed of the clock at exactly the time it stopped. He thought that maybe the dream was caused by the fact that the clock stopped ticking. But that still didn't explain how his dream could "see" that it stopped at 4:30.

Dunne writes: "If someone had told me the story, I'd have responded that the entire Episode, from beginning to end, including the "awakening" and adjusting of the clock, was only dreamed. But I couldn't give myself that answer. I knew exactly that I had been awake, gotten up and saw the clock on the cupboard".

He had his second time-shift experience in the coastal town of Sorrento, Italy. One morning he lay in bed and asked himself what time it might be. He felt too tired to get up and look at his pocket watch outside of his mosquito net on a table. He remembered his first experience and asked himself whether he might be able to see the watch with "clairvoyance" and so he closed his eyes and focused on the question of what time it is. He fell into a half sleep while remaining aware of his situation. A Vision of his watch appeared, standing upright about a meter in front of his nose, surrounded by daylight and a dense, white fog that filled the rest of his perceptual field. The hour hand was pointed at exactly 8:00, the minute hand was swinging between 12 and 1 and the seconds hand was too blurred to recognize. He had the feeling he would wake up if he looked too closely, and so treated the swinging minute hand like the needle of a compass, by defining the center of the swing. That let him determine that it was around 8:02. He opened his eyes and got his watch. He was wide awake when he discovered that it was exactly 8:02. "This time there was no excuse. I had to conclude that I had some strange ability "to see" through space and time. But I was still wrong" (I believe that Mr.

Dunne is remote viewing in this instance, but Dunne disagrees and sees even this as time travel).

Finally, Dunne experienced something which did not fit into his explanations on clairvoyance. In January 1901 he was in Alassio, Italy. There he dreamed one night that he is in Fashoda, near the town of Khartoum at the northern part of the Nile River. "It was an entirely normal dream, without any intense or bright scenes, except for one: The sudden appearance of three Men that had come from the south. They looked extremely scruffy, dressed in Khaki so faded, that it looked like the fabric of a sack. Their faces under the dusty helmets were sunburned, almost black. They looked like the men who had accompanied me on a recent tour in South Africa. I wondered why they had traveled the whole way from South Africa to Sudan and I asked them. They assured me that they had traveled from South Africa and had been through a terrible time. One of them said he had almost died of yellow fever. The rest of the dream was unimportant,".

At the time, Dunne received the Daily Telegraph newspaper from England. At breakfast the next morning, he read the following headline" "*Cap to Cairo. Expedition at Khartoum. From our special correspondent in Khartoum, Thursday, 5 P.M. The Daily Telegraph Expedition has arrived at Khartoum after a magnificent Journey*". In another part of the newspaper he read that the Expedition was led by a man named M. Lionel Decle. He remembered reading the day before, that one of the three men had died a day earlier, not by yellow fever but another illness. He didn't know if that was true or whether there were three group leaders. He had heard years before that M. Lionel Decle thought about a trans-continental trip, but had no idea whether this plan had been carried out. The Expedition had arrived one day before the information was published in London. As the newspaper had to be delivered from London to Alassio, Italy, which could take some time in those days, it must have happened long before the dream. The dream happened the night before the newspaper arrived. Dunne concluded that he did not "astral travel" to Khartoum. But he remained open to what the explanation might be.

His next paranormal experience was the dramatic one that would clarify it all. Quoted from the book:

"In the spring of 1902 I was encamped with the 6th Mounted Infantry near the ruins of Lindley, in the (then) Orange Free State. We had just come off trek, and mails and newspapers arrived but rarely.

There, one night, I had an unusually vivid and rather unpleasant dream.

I seemed to be standing on high ground — the upper slopes of some spur of a hill or mountain.

The ground was of a curious white formation. Here and there in this were little fissures, and from these jets of vapor were spouting upward. In my dream I recognized the place as an island of which I had dreamed before — an island which was in imminent peril from a volcano. And, when I saw the vapor spouting from the ground, I gasped: "It's the island! Good Lord, the whole thing is going to blow up". For I had memories of reading about Krakatoa, where the sea, making its way into the heart of a volcano through a submarine crevice, flushed into steam, and blew the whole mountain to pieces. Forthwith I was seized with a frantic desire to save the four thousand (I knew the number) unsuspecting inhabitants.

Obviously, there was only one way of doing this, and that was to take them off in ships. There followed a most distressing nightmare, in which I was at a neighboring island, trying to get the incredulous French authorities to dispatch vessels of every and any description to remove the inhabitants of the threatened island. I was sent from one official to another; and finally woke myself by my own dream exertions, clinging to the heads of a team of horses drawing the carriage of one "Monsieur le Maire," who was going out to dine, and wanted me to return when his office would be open next day. All through the dream the number of the people in danger obsessed my mind. I repeated it to everyone I met, and, at the moment of waking, I was shouting to Monsieur le Maire "Listen ! four thousand people will be killed unless.... "

I am not certain now when we received our next batch of papers but, when they did come, the Daily Telegraph was amongst them, and, on opening the centre sheet, this is what met my eyes :

VOLCANO DISASTER MARTINIQUE ; TOWN SWEPT AWAY ;AN AVALANCHE OF FLAME ; PROBABLE LOSS OF OVER 40,000 LIVES

BRITISH STEAMER BURNT

One of the most terrible disasters in the annals of the world has befallen the once prosperous town of St. Pierre, the commercial capital of the French island of Martinique in the West Indies. At eight o'clock on Thursday morning the volcano Mont Pelee which had been quiescent for a century, etc., etc. —

But there is no need to go over the story of the worst eruption in modern history.

In another column of the same paper was the following, the headlines being somewhat smaller :

A MOUNTAIN EXPLODES

There followed the report of the schooner Ocean Traveller, which had been obliged to leave St. Vincent owing to a fall of sand from the volcano there, and had subsequently been unable to reach St. Lucia owing to adverse currents opposite the ill-fated St. Pierre. The paragraph contained these words :

When she was about a mile off, the volcano Mont Pelee exploded.

The narrator subsequently described how the mountain seemed to split open all down the side.   Needless to say, ships were busy for some time after, removing survivors to neighbouring islands. There is one remark to be made here.

The number of people declared to be killed was not, as I had maintained throughout the dream, 4,000, but 40,000. I was out by a nought. But, when I read the paper, I read, in my haste, that number as 4,000; and, in telling the story subsequently, I always spoke of that printed figure as having been 4,000 ; and I did not know it was really 40,000 until I copied out the paragraph fifteen years later.

Now, when the next batch of papers arrived, these gave more exact estimates of what the actual loss of life had been ; and I discovered that the true figure had nothing in common with the arrangement of fours and noughts I had both dreamed of, and gathered from the first report. So my wonderful " clairvoyant" vision had been wrong in its most insistent particular! But it was clear that its wrongness was likely to prove a matter just as important as its rightness. For whence, in the dream, had I got that idea of 4,000?"

Dunne realized he got the number from newspapers he had read later.

But before he came to that realization, he suspected he might be suffering from Paramnesia. In that case he'd never had the dream but only thought he did, while reading the newspaper. The same could apply to his Vision of the travelers from Capetown to Cairo. Paramnesia is one of the explanations that "skeptics" offer, to debunk any experience of time travel. But the more he thought about both experiences, the more he understood that these dreams were exactly what one would expect after reading those two reports. Entirely normal dreams, influenced by what had been read. "How could I be sure that these dreams were no false memories that arose from reading the articles?" he wondered. At this point he was sure that he was not astral travelling, remote viewing or receiving telepathic messages from the people at those places. His dreams were obviously influenced by the reading of the reports themselves, so only three explanations remained: Paramnesia, a highly unlikely telepathic connection to journalists at the Daily Telegraph or Time Travel.

Fortunately, Dunne's next experience obliterated the "Paramnesia" Theory. He was now meticulously adhering to writing a Dream Journal. He wrote down every dream he had, in great detail. Over time, he found many dreams in his Journal, that he had later read in newspapers. He couldn't blame it on false memory because he had written it all down.

This was the dream that excluded all theories except time travel:

In 1904 Dunne stayed at the Hotel Scholastika, Aachensee (Aachen Lake) in Austria. The Hotel still exists today. A strange synchronicity: I spent a few days at the same Hotel in the same year I was reading J.W. Dunnes book. What are the odds?

He dreamed he was walking between two fields, alongside two iron railings. His attention was attracted by a Horse that was standing in the left field. The horse was acting crazy, lashing out and making noise. Nervously Dunne looked at the railing to see if there was an opening through which the Horse could enter. There was none so he continued on his way. A few moments later he heard hooves trampling behind him. He looked behind himself and to his dismay the angry Horse had somehow come through the railing and was running toward him at great speed. The dream turned into a nightmare and Dunne ran like a rabbit. The path ended and lead to a wooden staircase upwards that he tried to reach with all his power. Then the dream ended.

On the next day in waking life, Dunne went fishing with his brother at a river that runs from the Aachen Lake. While his eyes were gazing at the river, his brother suddenly called out "Look at that Horse!" Looking across the river he saw the Horse from his dream. It was the same scene as in the dream with only few differences in detail. The fields with a fenced path were there. The horse was behaving just like in the dream. The wooden stairs at the end of the path were there. They led to a Bridge that crossed the river. But the fences were small and made of wood and the fields looked small and mundane, unlike the dream where they looked huge and wide. In waking Life, the Horse looked small and harmless rather than the gigantic monster from the dream. The Horses behavior still made him nervous. Finally, the horse was in the "wrong field" on the right side, if he had walked the path to the stairs. Dunn began telling his brother about the dream, but abruptly stopped because the Horse really was behaving strangely and he wanted to make sure it couldn't escape.

Just like in the dream, he skeptically examined the railing. Just like in the dream, he could see no opening through which the horse could escape. He told his brother "The Horse won't be able to get through it". He continued fishing but a few seconds later his brother said "Look out!" Just like in the dream, the Horse had inexplicably left the field. It had probably jumped. Just like in the dream it was now running toward the wooden stairs. It ran past the stirs and jumped directly into the river, moving toward the two men. They picked up rocks and moved away from the river, preparing to defend themselves. The end was tame, as the Horse got out of the water, briefly looked at the two and galloped down the road.

Dunne found that most of his dreams were not Visions of distant futures but *regular dreams* containing typical illogic and distorted details that dreams have. The only odd thing about them is that they happened "on the wrong night", an evening before the event, not after.

Dunne asked himself whether there were other people having these experiences. Out of this question he developed a series of experiments and studies that culminated in the popular 1927 book "An Experiment in Time". The book attracted the attention of the Press, Science and Public. Famous people of the time, such as Albert Einstein and H.G. Wells wrote commentaries on the book and corresponded with the author.

A large portion of the book is research around physics, perception and consciousness. Another part of it addresses experiences as described above. And another part presents the results of his studies. I've summarized some other insights I gleaned from the book in the next paragraphs:

- If you wish to research your dreams for time travel, *then write each dream down in detail.* This increases dream awareness and serves as a later *reference* to *discover* a time anomaly. If you can't remember a dream, then try instead to remember the first thing you thought of, after awakening. Then ask yourself why that's the first thought. Now you might be able to catch the thread of your dream and remember.

- Dream-Trips into the Past are less noticed than those into the Future, because the mind automatically assumes that the dream was "caused" through past events. But that's not always true. Sometimes consciousness simply travels to those past locations.

- In Dunne's experiments with test subjects, not a single precognitive dream was discovered, if the dreams hadn't been written down before, read later and recognized as predictive. This didn't surprise Dunne, as none of these people had the habit to compare their daily life with previous dreams. Only when people *deliberately research* the subject, they discover that they have many more future-dreams than they knew. Most test subjects already noticed specific results three to twelve days into the Experiment.

- We often experience things in life of which we forget that we dreamed about. But a later read of dream journals reveals that we are in fact time travelers. I'll say that again, just to make it clearer: *Writing dream journals will eventually reveal that you are already a time traveler and that you can "see into the future" as well as travel to the past.*

- Dunne had the best results in precognitive dreaming when the routine of daily life was interrupted. On vacation, far away from home or in unusual situations he had the sharpest dream recall and the most precognitive dreams. I can confirm this from my own experiences.

- *Every* test person had precognitive dreams. Most weren't aware of it until they compared their day to day experience with their dream journals. Amazingly, some didn't even realize it then! Dunne cites the example of a woman who was so skeptical that she did not see a connection between climbing a roof today and having dreamed of climbing a roof the night before. If there is anything keeping people from awakening, it's their own stubbornness.

- Dunne also attempted to try precognition in a waking state, without dreams. In one instance he went to a library, took a book into his hand and tried to receive an image about what he was about to read (in the future). "These exercises showed me that if a person could calm their attention and focus on the task, they could produce the "effect" (precognition) in a waking state". Dunne said it was more difficult to do so in a waking state because most energy is used to delete images from the past. Dunne says that in the waking-state experiments he was looking for the barrier thar separates knowledge of past from knowledge of future. "The strange thing was, that such a Barrier didn't exist". All that needs to be done, according to Dunne is to stop any obvious thought of the past, then the future would appear in dissociated "flashes" (dissociated meaning separate from normal thoughts). I agree with Dunn on this—there is nothing stopping anyone from seeing "the future". It's only a matter of clearing the mind.

- What is the influence of my precognitive dream on the event taking place later? Is there a connection? Would I have even experienced it if I hadn't dreamed it beforehand? Is consciousness assembling my next day or days while I am sleeping? Or is it really a dream of something that I would later experience, regardless? Does writing my dream down the next morning support or block the later event? The book doesn't answer these questions. And I won't answer them either but give them to you as food for thought.

- The final part of the book is about experiments that Dunne made in cooperation with Oxford University. During this Phase Dunne began discerning between normal dreams, precognitive dreams and retro-cognitive dreams. Not every dream interpreted as "precognitive" is one. For example, if you are dreaming that you are visiting a lecture and then you later visit the lecture, that is not a precognitive dream if you a) planned visiting the lecture before you had a dream or b) visit lectures on a regular basis anyway. It would be a precognitive dream if you had never visited a lecture and then find yourself unexpectedly visiting one. Your dream is also not necessarily "precognitive" if you are invited to a lecture and in that moment remember the dream and then tell yourself "Right. I'll go there to confirm the dream". But even without such instances, you still have plenty of real precognitive dreams and you notice them if you pay attention.

I share all of this with you, to show that *you are already time travelling*. It's not something you need to "learn", it's more a question of noticing. Time is malleable and flexible and nothing like "society" thinks it is.

While writing the 2003 version of this book, I had a few time-anomalous dreams. That's because, what you focus on, becomes more real. I had a dream that mixed memories of the day before, subconscious worries and precognitive Elements. I share this so that you know that most dreams aren't purely one thing or another.

In the dream, someone followed me through the city with a gun. The city was a mixture of several I had been to the weeks before. Strangely enough, the person with the gun had stolen it out of a car. I was also being followed by a strange woman that felt more threatening than the man with the gun. The city images were memory-bits of previous weeks, the people following me were people I was wary of in real life. The precognitive Element appeared when I received a phone call from a Mrs. Wenger. On the phone she asked me to pay the invoice for the gun that I had bought. I tried explaining to her, that I wouldn't pay for the gun because it had been stolen from me (in the non-logic typical of dreams – actually it wasn't me owning a gun, I was being followed by a person who had stolen a gun). Mrs. Wenger called several times throughout the dream. Once I even heard a whisper announce: "A call from Mrs. Wenger incoming". In waking life, I didn't know any Mrs. Wenger, so I forgot the dream quickly. It was only later in the day when my Partner got a call from a Mrs. Wenger and she told me her name, that I remembered the dream. It had been the third time that month, that I had a precognitive dream insight. But what did it mean? Back then, I didn't know. And the first time I wrote the last paragraph was 2002. Now it's 2020, and retrospectively, I realize that the dream was trying to warn me of Mrs. Wenger. It turned out 10 years later that my ex-partners decision to work for Mrs. Wenger would lead down a negative path for her. Not for me, as I broke up with her long before that. But back then I was just not aware enough to decipher the dream. But that's not something to worry about. If this ex-girlfriend of mine went down a negative path, that's a consequence of many of her decisions over time, not the result of me misunderstanding one dream. I say this because people stuck in false guilt would see it that way.

Since 2002, my ability to *feel the meaning* of dreams has greatly improved. This is mostly due to the fact that I and my wife share our dreams almost every morning. Such daily repetition, increases dream awareness. That is, she usually shares hers as I don't have many. The reason I don't have many is because my subconscious is no longer processing that much, because I quit suppressing events, images and emotions years ago. Precognitive insights therefore rarely come in dreams anymore, but they do come as intuitive flashes in waking life.

An exception to this was a dream I had just a week ago: I dreamed that I was travelling on a bright and fast train and that my wife was getting off the train but had forgotten her phone. I was wondering how I could contact her if she'd left her phone with me. I soon forgot about the dream because it didn't mean much at first sight. Then, two days ago, she actually left her phone at home while going out, which is uncharacteristic of her (the first time it ever happened). Then, today, as I write this, she did it again. That's twice in a row whereas she'd never done it in many years before. And I had actually pre-cognized this in a dream. But what did it mean? Why did I dream it? How was it relevant? At first, I thought it meant nothing. But if a thing means nothing, we are unlikely to dream about it, much less remember the dream.

Now, a few weeks later I can add this paragraph, because I know what the incident meant. She began pursuing an entirely different career path than before. The precognition was *symbolic* in this instance. She did something uncharacteristic in the dream. Then in waking life. Then, even more so, by radically altering her career path. But the energy whirl that led to that decision, was already developing several weeks prior, and I picked up on that in a dream. Her leaving the phone at home twice, something she really never did, indicated a change in attitude and personality. In other words, signs and omens really do precede big changes.

Time Travel Journal

Are you reading this book for personal entertainment, education or because you genuinely wish to time travel? If its time travel, then get a Dream Journal. That's any Notebook in which you write down what you dreamt. That'll get you real, *tangible results*, beyond all the mumbo jumbo.

I became a Lucid Dreamer thanks to my Dream Journal. I'd have never remembered certain dreams without it. In remembering those dreams while dreaming, I became lucid within the dreams. In becoming more aware of my dreams, I became more aware within my dreams. If you value your dreams, you write them down and then they'll value you. It is not possible to get more clarity without investing attention. If it's specific hard proof you are looking for, you can't get around this. If you don't care about proving time travel to yourself and lazily take my word for it, then you can do without dream journaling. Write your dreams, your waking life pre-cogs and when you intuited or remote viewed something. Write down other unexplained occurrences. This is how to make it happen more often, with greater control. The act of writing is taking control of what would otherwise remain vague or fleeting.

Deja-Vu Experiences, sometimes come from having previewed a scenario in dreamscape. Sometimes you visit a place in waking life and you say "Oh yeah, I've been here before... on Dreamscape!"

James Dunne was right. Without writing some of my dreams down, I'd have never made sense of it all. And when the rigid borders between dreamlife and waking become more fluid, some strange things can happen. For example, a few months ago I had an important meeting regarding work for a very influential group of people. I dreamed about this meeting a few weeks before it was scheduled, and in my dream, it didn't turn out the way I had hoped. My presentation had been vague. I hadn't asked what was most important to these people. So, I used the precognition, to *change* the future. I went to the meeting, asking "What are the three most important things for you?" before starting my own presentation. And that made all the difference. I got the four-week contract and it was a phenomenal experience.

Viewing my Dream Journal taught me how the conscious mind tends to censor and forget. It will delete anything that doesn't match its beliefs. One of these being paranormal abilities. But if you write them down, you have evidence that the mind cannot censor or forget. Certain knowledge is state-dependent. When someone is drunk, they'll do things that they forget the next morning. But once they are drunk again, they'll remember and laugh about what they did last time they were drunk. That doesn't only apply to being drunk, it applies to all states and roles you occupy in a lifetime. I wrote my 2006 book "Parallel Universe of Self" based on realizations around identity-shifting.

Do not underestimate your minds ability to forget, censor and rationalize. Write down when you experience something special. The mind tries to make things mundane, as if life weren't utterly miraculous. To progress as a time traveler, you require success-experiences. Write down your dreams after you wake up. Or at least, talk about what you dreamed after awakening. And at the very least, re-run it in your mind.

You don't want all things happening in your mind to be vague and fleeting, you want clarity.

Doing so would be a new habit for most of you. You might already have other morning habits. If so, you need to determine whether learning more about consciousness is important enough for you. Re-running your dreams has multiple benefits, access to time travel is only one of them.

3

The Center of Infinity

"I know neither who I am nor where I am, but I've never been this happy "- Typical sentiment of a Time Traveler

All experience of past and future can be perceived here-now. This present moment is the point at which every timeline and place converge. Time exists in Consciousness. Memories of the past and imaginings of the future...when do they exist? Now, in the mind. The core of consciousness is outside of time and space, because consciousness can observe time and space. What *you are* is infinite and eternal. Nothing is hidden to the Source which you are part of. Anything you can imagine and much more can be experienced. Your core is at the center of Infinity and from this perspective, you can obtain information and experience about any reality, any dimension, any time and any universe. You can also be present anywhere, with all your senses.

Time Travel, Remote Viewing, ESP (Extrasensory Perception) and other „paranormal abilities" are easy to have, from this point of view. Seen from a common viewpoint it may seem „difficult ". You see yourself as a human being within a big, mysterious Universe. This is what you were taught in school, and the concept sank in, without your detection because you didn't know any better. But what if this viewpoint is exactly that...just a viewpoint and not „absolute truth "? Another viewpoint you were not taught, is that the Universe is within you rather than you being within it. What if that were true? I believe it is. And I believe the reason you don't see it that way is because you think it might intrude on your comfortable experience as a „human on Planet Earth ".

Many are surprised when they have a „paranormal "or „divine "experience because they are "humans having a divine experience". But what if you are actually something divine that is having a temporary human experience? Is your soul within you or are you within a soul?

You pretend to know about the nature of reality, but you won't be able to honestly answer these fundamentally important questions:

Where are you? Yes, where are you? Where exactly? People invest a lot of energy to define just where they are. As „smart and educated "as you are, you might say

„Well, I'm right here on Earth "but then I'd ask you: Where is that? And maybe you'd answer

„It's in the Universe ". And where is that? And you'll say

„Well...uh...whatever. Let's go grab something to eat ".

Space is a creation of the mind. Points of orientation, even though useful, are inventions of the mind. You can only know where you are, compared to something else, within duality. If there is an East, then you can define a West and you can determine where you are in relation to that polarity. We see other Planets, so we can say that we are here on this Planet (thank goodness! For a moment I thought I didn't know where I am!) The same goes for Galaxies, Universes and all else. Maybe you are nowhere and everywhere....

Who are you? Yes, who are you in fact? People invest a lot of energy to define who they are. That's fun and useful for the remainder of ones stay on Earth. But in moments of honesty you can feel it: You don't have the slightest clue who you are. You don't even know exactly where you are from. You have told yourself many times. Every time you meet another person you say „I am "and „My name is ". But do you know with total certainty who you really are? Your name is only a label. Do you have memories of where you were before you were here? And before that? And before that? And before that? Maybe you come from nowhere and are going nowhere and maybe you are nobody. Who knows? To quote a well-known movie: *"The matrix cannot tell you who you are"*.

Time and Identity are inventions of consciousness. Consciousness is all that is. Advanced individuals realize that and start asking more intelligent questions than „Who am I? "They ask questions such as „Who would I like to be? "or „What would have to happen so that I can be that? "

Can you see that your „knowledge "is empty, rehearsed, conditioned? That's how your current „reality "was created: Certain concepts are repeated over and over, until they are perceived as „true ". Have you ever noticed how you begin perceiving things after someone talks about them?

And now you experience yourself as a Being that lives on earth and is someone. But maybe you already know all of this. Maybe you feel deep within, that nothing is as it seems.

Time Travel, as you've always dreamed of (admit it), is possible. That's why so many have a longing for it. Or do you really think you are given a desire without the potential to make it come true?

AS WHO you approach this topic, determines what you perceive and experience. If you approach it as a normal, limited body-mind-mechanism, looking from bottom to top, then "Time Travel" will require hard, decades long Training...until you realize, it's not possible. But if you take on the viewpoint of Infinite Being that is part of all-that-is, then the task does not seem quite as daunting.

The paradox is, you already know how to time travel because the *real you* already exists outside of time. The person I am writing or talking to now, is the person who will never learn or understand any of this, because that person is just a limited mind of a human Being. That's its purpose: To be a limited mind. So why teach you something that you will never learn? By focusing on the topic for a while, pretending to be learning it, the part of you that has always known, awakens. This part of you needn't be taught. This true, non-physical self comes to the foreground and participates in your research. From this perspective, time travel is merely a matter of Focus.

We won't be needing machines to time travel. We'll be talking about some of the alleged technology out there, but we won't need it. Anyone can travel and perceive from the comfort of their homes. "I wanted to time travel for real, not just in my Imagination" you might be protesting. But time travel, the way I teach it, is not just closing your eyes and imagining that you are in a the 17th or 25th Century. It is possible to travel through space and time with consciousness and perceive what is happening at any given place or time, without the use of Imagination. The ability is called Remote Viewing and is quite common. So common is the ability that U.S. Military has invested hundreds of Millions of Dollars in Research on Remote Viewing for Spying and Intelligence purposes. Nobody would spend that much money if it were only a fantasy. Once you understand that you can perceive across space, you realize that you can also perceive across time. You are able to be present at different times and experience them as if you were personally there, without Imagination. It's one of our underdeveloped superpowers.

I have been able to travel out of body at will, since my childhood. On these trips, time was experienced as non-linear. I began experimenting and discovered that, in an out-of-body state it is easy to project oneself into other times. I observed that there are different timelines (different pasts and futures). I enjoyed the parallel worlds of other timelines. I not only experienced parallel universes in out-of-body-states but also in night dreams. To quote from another book of mine (Essays on Creating Reality Book 4):

*In my early twenties I had the recurring dream of being a professional soccer player in Europe. Every time I had the dream, I **remembered previous dreams** on that timeline, complete with recurring cast and scenery. My challenge on that timeline was establishing myself as a first-team player. I was a substitute and was sometimes relegated to play for the smaller league B-Team. When I spent too much time playing for the B-Team, I got worried that I'd lose market value and skill and might get stuck there. This was not just your usual vague dream, there were **hundreds** of dreams in that reality and they all followed a logical sequence (unlike regular dreams). I knew it was a **parallel universe** because both the soccer club and the town it was in looked and felt **slightly different** than the same club and town in **this** reality. Because of these "dreams", I became* *interested in the Club and its soccer matches in **this** reality. Pay attention to the things that fascinate you in this reality – maybe that's because they are your fully developed career in another. In the parallel world, some of the players were the same, some looked slightly different, and some of my co-players were completely unknown in this reality. The Manager, was the same in both worlds. The Club overall was less successful in the other world. I played at a pro-level for only a few years, happy to have reached a pro-level but knowing my body couldn't sustain A-Team physique any longer.*

*One day, in **this** reality, I was invited to temporarily work at this soccer club. This was years after the dreams had faded away. Nonetheless, I understood that as the parallel reality, **dripping into** this one. If I chose to pursue that path more deeply, I could merge the two realities or even enter another timeline. The existence of "parallel universes" struck me the most intensely when I entered their training grounds for the first time in this reality. It was one big, **exhilarating Deja-vu experience.** Everything was familiar because I had spent so much time here in a parallel universe. While the facilities and rooms were not exactly the same as in the parallel life, some things were an exact match. I knew where the offices were. I knew what elevator to take to get to them. I knew what door would lead to the parking garage. I knew where the players locker rooms were before I was shown. When a parallel Universe drips into this one, it's a most peculiar feeling. How could I know so much about facilities I was visiting for the first time in this reality? This was one of the most paranormal experiences I have had.*

*I did not share the story with anyone, because it's kind of hard to explain. **"Yeah…I know this place. I worked here for many*** *years, in a parallel universe". My engagement for this soccer club in this world was fairly short as I chose not to pursue this path. But from this experience, I learned another important thing: If you wish to pursue, enter or solidify a certain reality, you must FEEL it. There's a certain*

vibration,

tone,

atmosphere,

mood,

quality

ambience

*that goes along with every reality. For example, now, while I am writing about it, I remember that company, both in this and in the parallel world. The company has **a distinct feel to it**. Every reality has a distinct mood that differs from others. If I kept dwelling on it, I'd gradually start entering it again. It's a process of vibratory habituation. And I'd presumably soon get a phone call from them. Have you ever noticed how you talk or think about someone who you haven't thought about in a while and the next day they call you? That's because whatever you put your attention on, you start vibrating with and as. That means, **if you want nothing more to do with a certain reality, stop feeding it attention**. It's a common problem in society that, when "problems" occur, people get all excited, worried, upset about it…which gives the problem even more reality.*

I'm aware of a few other parallel lives, some less desirable, some more. But currently, I'm in a happy place in this reality, so I don't give the other lives much thought. Should I someday seek change, I'll know how to change my frequency to merge with another reality.

*As I write in my book "Parallel Universes of Self", you can do that too. It's not that difficult. What is needed? Well, you need to first **know what you prefer** and then you need to look for the feeling or **mood** of that. This is much easier when you're in an open state. If your daily life is already full to the brim with fixed ideas, errands, habits, issues, desires, aversions, beliefs…. then you'll have a hard time feeling anything outside of your habitual comfort zone. If you wish to experience something new, you must first be able to feel something new.*

There are many ways to feel something new. Typically, a person would…

go to a new place,

meet new people, think and visualize new things,

learn new things or

do new things

to shake up their energy field a little. But if you want things to stay as they are, or improve and change more slowly, then reduce the new. It's up to you. You have more control than you know, all by what you choose to dwell on. You have many parallel lives. The reason you know a lot about a subject that you haven't really experienced in this life and the reason you are fascinated by certain things, might be because another version of you is living them. Follow the fascination and you'll start getting drawn into another life.

This knowledge has allowed me to radically alter my life several times already in "this" life. But it's not really "this" life. I've merely shifted timelines a few times, shifting from life to life. I've lived long-term in four completely different countries and cultures with completely different sets of friends and lifestyles. I'm fascinated that some people maintain the same place of living, the same house, the same job and the same circle of acquaintances their entire life. Why? Because it's easier. It's comforting to know that nothing unexpected will ever happen. But people who are too extreme in this, will find that the world around them changes and they hold on to the familiar too tightly, they'll get swept away. So, change before you have to.

*Your life is a habit of feeling. If you want something different to happen, first change how you **feel** (about life and yourself in general or about specific things).*

An exercise in Timelessness

Before we venture into Time Travel, it is wise to first experience a state of timelessness. If you learn that there is no such thing as time, then time travel is a piece of cake.

When someone titles an email URGENT!!!!!! I know it's a lie. I like to delete those without reading. We know it's a lie because marketers and politicians use it to sell their wares. Time, Schedules, Work, Goals and Purpose are great tools to live consciously. But too much reliance on them makes you unhappy because as Souls we are Timeless. Our lives are too determined by the idea of time and these exercises help to reduce that. That doesn't mean you'll be apathetic, miss important appointments or lose track of daily life. It means that you leave the rat race. You will feel consciousness expanded.

Exercise 1: Walk in Timelessness

Temporarily disconnect from time, intent, priority, urgency, need. You do so consciously, not randomly. Have you ever noticed that when you are walking, you usually have a Goal that you are walking toward? That awareness is not entirely with your present surroundings or the walk itself, but on places to arrive at and things you have to do? Or have you noticed how you walk with a specific purpose such as weight loss or taking selfies? All that is fine, but it's not timeless. Or that you walk while thinking of errands to take care of? Or that you walk and put more interest on specific objects and people than others? None of that is entirely timeless.

The timeless walk, is walking without Goal, Purpose, Emphasis. You don't have to arrive anywhere, return anywhere and you are not fulfilling any task. You are just walking. Period. You don't combine your timeless walk with grocery shopping or taking the Dog out. Should you happen to end up in a grocery store, that's fine, as long as it wasn't the goal. Nor do you intentionally walk a path you are familiar with or prefer. Timeless walking is without expectation or plan. And there is no official time limit.

You might look at things you don't normally look at. That calms the mind because its outside of habit. Have you ever noticed manhole covers in the street? If you've been a slave to the rat-race, I'd guess you never gave them any attention at all, because the mind calculates everything in terms of "what benefit I get". As there is no recorded benefit of looking at manhole covers, the mind ignores them and whips you into an endless array of survival-based urgencies. "Go there! Do this! Think that! Hurry up!"

How many times have you looked at the clouds while walking? What about looking more closely at those trees, even touching them? Let go of yourself, get over yourself. There is a "higher order" that is guiding you. This same "higher order" lets plants, trees, vegetables, fruits grow all by themselves, without effort, strain, purpose or construct. When you stop over-analyzing, higher-self takes over and you enter a more conscious state. When the first layers of impatience and boredom fall off, a deeper peace and contentment arise. In this peace, new ideas may develop. However: You are not walking "in order to gain more relaxation and creativity". That's purpose again! You see how the mind keeps grasping for reason and purpose? It's a neurotic mind, terrified of any moment of genuine tranquility. Walk without having a reason for it. There is nothing urgent to do. Allow spontaneity. Notice how the mind keeps trying to make sense of everything or to get you to "go the right way". Observe the monkey-mind with Humor and just keep walking. The timeless state being referred to here, cannot be expressed with words.

Exercise 2: More Timelessness

A lot of people talk about being "beyond time" and "transcending time", but few aput it into practice. In this exercise, I'd like you to spend an entire week without Time.

That's a paradox isn't it. If something is defined as "A Week", how can it be timeless? Well, you might as well be Timeless forever, if that makes sense. During the exercise (or that designated "Week"), get rid of:

1.   Your Watch or the Time-Display on Your Phone

2.   All Clocks and Watches in your Surroundings. Make sure to do your best to avoid seeing time indicators.

3.   If you see a time indicator in public, deliberately ignore it.

4.   Stop using the words "time", "clock", "o'clock", "watch" and anything else related. Don't say "We'll meet at 8 o'clock", and don't say "I am experimenting with being timeless". Since you assume that you know nothing of time, you wouldn't be experimenting with time. Just drop the whole concept entirely.

5.   You will probably have to reduce TV and Internet during this week, because these things keep affirming the idea of time.

6.   Don't plan any activities according to time, but act spontaneously on what you'd prefer to do, take care of or experience from moment to moment.

7.   It might be necessary to take a week off of work for this, unless you can manage being timeless at work.

Experience of timelessness is worth much more than the intellectual understanding that "time is only a construct". You can now start using the concept of time again in order to align with societies norms, but I recommend you don't do it to the point of being trapped in time.

Being Everywhere and Nowhere

If you practiced the "Exercises in Timelessness" you experienced a state beyond time. Let's now explore a state beyond space. Consciousness itself is beyond Time and Space, not confined to a particular time or location. Peoples reality is defined (limited) by talking about "where" they are. But, just like time, location is an arbitrary construct of mind.

Where are you? You might say you are in Ireland. So where is that? Europe. And where is that? The world. And where is that? The solar system. And where is that? The Universe. And where is that? The honest answer: I don't know. You don't know where you are because the "where-ness" of a thing is a creation-of-consciousness, only valid within a limited context. A specific place can only be defined in comparison to other specific places. The Infinite Self is not bound by time and space. That's why consciousness is able to perceive across time and space. This Self, in its most blissful state, is witness to time and space. People keep affirming ideas about Space and Time. That's the World-Self trying to feel comfortable and maintain some semblance of knowledge and sanity in the this vast Omniverse.

An Exercise Beyond Space

This is an exercise to expand Awareness. Spend at least one week in which you avoid referencing or talking about Space,

Place and Distances. When you catch yourself doing that, let go or lead the conversation elsewhere. Act as if all-that-is, exists right here, simultaneously. It actually does, but the Mind filters all of that out, selects and creates distance and difference in order to experience things on a timeline. If we didn't continually define time and space, we'd have a hard time living on Earth. It's the urge to experience all-that-is in small segments that creates time and space. Experiencing everything at once could be overwhelming. And that's neither good nor bad, it's just the mechanics of life, two different ways of perceiving things – either in their infinite splendor or piece by piece. You don't have to take this exercise so far that you float away, but loosening your rigid focus on time and location just a little is enough to expand your sense of lightness and freedom.

The exercise asks you to ignore the following concepts for a whole week:

Where

From Where

Here

There

Over There

Behind

In Front Of,

Right

Left

At

In

On

Above

Below

I am from

How far

Get To

Go To

long way

short way

Travel

and similar.

You still move through space, but know nothing about it. Take this exercise so far that you don't even know what the exercise is about. If Location does not exist, there is no reason to negate it.

At first you might notice how dependent you and others are on concepts of Space, continually re-creating the idea (hint: If something is real, as in ultimate-reality, it doesn't have to be reaffirmed all the time, it exists regardless of our confirmation). During this week, even if others are referencing location, you do not have to respond. Nor do you have to share the exercise you are doing, as some people might question your sanity (they take their "place" in the Universe for granted, as if that's entirely sane).

You might notice unique feelings of lightness or "highs" – these come from loosening the minds rigid grip.

After the week is over, reflect on what you experienced. What is it like when references to place and distance are removed? Does reality feel less separate, deeper? Did your perception of shapes and colors change? Did you notice anything else?

Once you realize consciousness is everywhere and nowhere, you no longer use space as your center and means of orientation, but rather your Soul, Energy, Being. It then does not so much matter "where" you are but *who* you are.

Bridges Across Time

Having practiced timelessness, lets now practice some time travel. I have developed these exercises for "warm up" before you learn the Time Travel Method in a later chapter.

Imagine that it's possible to communicate with past and future versions of yourself. Imagine, for example, that you are sending the 15-year-old version of you, the message "*everything will be alright*". Try that right now. Remember who you were when you were 15 and tell that person: "*Everything will be alright*".

If you send your past-self messages, information and love you will receive messages, information and love from your future self.

If you are in the habit of sending your past-self good messages, it follows that your present self is also receiving good things from your future self, because your present self is the past self from the viewpoint of your future self. If anything in this chapter gets confusing, please slow down and re-read the sentence, until its grasped.

I believe it is possible to get information from the future…from yourself, including useful information and to also receive actionable info from the past (again from yourself). Likewise, you are able to deliver information to both your past and future selves. All that is required is an awareness of these selves.

If you start sending your past-self energy and support today, there will be a version of you that has already been doing that for a while. If this resonates with you, try it for a few weeks or more. The quality of your life will improve.

Even if these were "only imagined", your quality of life improves because you will only be doing things that you'd prefer retrospectively.

How likely is it, that your future self would help you if you ask for support? Probably more likely than if you ask any stranger. You wouldn't deny yourself the support. So, create a way to communicate and get questions from your other selves, or use the following exercises:

Communication with a Past Self

Focus on a version of you from the past. See and feel what that version of you is seeing and feeling. In which environment is he/she is living and what he/she is doing?

Talk to this version of you, send thought-forms or Energy. Do so in a compassionate and encouraging mood and manner.

Communication with a Future Self

Imagine a future Self in a Scene in which he/she presumably resides. Modify the image to an ideal future.

Feel your connection to this version of you. Feel how he/she would never refuse you, because he/she *is* you.

Communicate. Ask Questions. Allow for answers.

These two exercises can be done mentally (imagination, intuition), verbally or in writing. If you enjoy building these bridges across time, you might want to do it more thoroughly than just described. Like this for example:

For a Meeting with myself I've turned off all phones, closed the curtains and lit a candle. I lie down, close my eyes and begin with soft and deep abdominal breathing until I feel silent and effortless. I visualize floating in a warm and cozy energy bubble. Maybe I feel my spine or forehead tingling and I start feeling much better. The energy bubble is floating through space. I look through the bubble, to the outside. I think of the past or future version of myself that I'd like to contact now. I breathe and keep awareness on that Person.

At the same time, I see a calendar in my mind's eye, that begins with today's date. I flip through the calendar to reach the date I am targeting. Maybe my past or future self-will mock me for using such complicated methods to reach him/her. No matter. Once I reach the intended date, I see the other version of Me, how he/she was at the time.

Initially, exercises like these take place in Imagination. With some practice and clarity of focus, the connection becomes clearer and *intuition replaces imagination*. I will perceive a person that seems to be separate from my current Self. I tell them what I'd like to say. Maybe I have wisdom to give or maybe I have questions. Don't assume that the past self is all ignorant and the future self all wise. We change many times throughout life, and have different versions, not necessarily better or worse. The past self may know things you have forgotten.

If you wish to give the session a therapeutic touch, then imagine giving the past self some advice. Then visualize the past self, following your advice and as a result, experiencing other results than what you remembered. This process is called "Changing History".

The past Self *wants to* communicate with you, not only you with him or her. Don't only ask questions, listen attentively. Initially the answers you receive are projected by your present-self. With some practice, you begin receiving other answers than you expected. That's when you have crossed the threshold from imagining to perceiving.

Once you are done with the session, return to the calendar and, in your mind's eye, flip the pages back to current time. Take a few deep breathes and center yourself. Open your eyes and make notes if you like.

Time is a perceptual filter that helps you experience life as a sequence of segments. In reality you *always have access to all experiences that you will ever have and have ever had.* That includes parallel lives and possibly past and future lives. But imagine the Chaos if you'd experience all of that now. You'd be unable to have any experiences in-detail. When a soul comes to Earth, intentionally limiting itself to this dense reality, it does so, so that it can experience in-detail, close up and intimate. A lot of people say "Live without Limits! There are no limits!", but actually incarnate Souls came here to experience those limits.

Do you feel that you do not have the energy and zest that you once had in life? Or that you might feel the energy if event X happens? Well, you can actually access those points in time right this moment. Merely remembering the time, you had energy, invites it back to be felt right now. Merely imagining the state, you will have when X happens, you feel better.

Communicating with the Future or Past are not the only Bridges across time. What follows is a list of possibilities. Any of these Bridges can open a number of amazing insights. Keep in mind that all these times exist in the now, simultaneously. They always have and always will exist at any time. Quieting the mind and intend to get there. The following descriptions are *examples*.

Present to Past

You remember a past event in which you were in trouble. You send the past-self emotional support and encouragement. "It's OK my friend. You'll get through this. I'm with you". You could also do therapy with the past-self (instead of making it responsible for how you feel today, which is the common delusion of "traditional therapy").

Present to Present

Step outside of yourself for a moment, and view yourself from there. One "you" stands up, the other stays sitting. Start talking to the person that is still sitting in that chair. It's strange to view yourself from the outside, right? But it's helpful. If you were this Persons Mentor, what would you tell him/her?

Present to Future

Close your eyes and imagine a future version of yourself and start talking to him or her. Any question is allowed. It's fine to idealize this future-you a little and it increases the chances of becoming that. Do you notice any difference between, say, the version of you in 10 years and a version of you 500 years in the future? Any similarities? What are the possibilities?

Past to Present

Imagine you are one of your past Identities. Take some time to really feel what it's like to be that past version of you. As this past-self, put attention on the present-self (future-self from his/her perspective). Try sending to or receiving information from that self. Is there something you knew as a child, forgotten later? Could you flow some of that forgotten stuff to the present (the future)? How does an energy flow past-to-present feel different from the flow present-to-past?

Past to Past

This one really expands your sense of self. Imagine a past version of you is communicating with another past version of you. The 10-year-old you might be talking to the 20-year-old you. If there are certain things you knew as a child that you have forgotten, and you can't seem to access them, then have the 10-year-old first give it to the 16-year-old. The 16-year-old can then pass it on to the 20-year-old and then to the present. That might make it easier to access lost info. Even more far out: You let your 500-year-old self remember the 10 000-year-old self. Did you have a self that long ago? Was that self on Earth, another Planet or Pre-Incarnate? Have fun with this.

Past to Future

Imagine how a past version of you stretches his/her hand far into the future to glean inspiration from there, without any involvement of the present Self. Or how your Million-year old self communicates to a self a Million years older. This one is quite amusing because it bypasses the present-self which you deem so much more important than the others, but its only one of many versions of you.

Future to Present

Take some time to relax and imagine yourself into being a future version of you. Maybe one in 5 years, 10 years or even 500 years. Being that future-self, look to your present-self (past-self, from that perspective). Would you like to give him/her advice? Help him/her in something? Can you tell the difference between *Future to Present* and *Present to Future?* Here you imply that it's the Future Self that intends to initiate communication, which is a whole different viewpoint than Present to Future. Most people who do this exercise will feel invigorated. Why? They've accessed an entirely different energy field.

Future to Past

See how your Future-Self, the more wise and experienced Self takes up contact with a past version of you. The advice your future self gives to your past self is probably even better than the advice your present self would give. Or perhaps the advice is not as good because that future self is too far away from that past self. I don't know, see for yourself. Done slowly and deliberately, this exercise, like others, has healing potential.

Future to Future

See how two future versions of you are enjoying communication. Perhaps the You in 20 years is talking to the You in 200 years. Or maybe they are talking about the present you. This might be the most enjoyable variation.

There is more to these "Bridges across time" than described in this section. I explain less and invite you to make your own experiences. Through contemplation on the Bridges, you develop time-flexibility, which is a prerequisite for time-travel.

Parallel Worlds Meditation

If I build a time machine and travel to 1950 where I accidentally kill my Grandmother while she was still a child, that means that my mother was never born, which means that I was never born. If I was never born, then I could have never built a time machine. Without having built a time machine, I couldn't have travelled to 1950 and accidentally killed my Grandmother. That means my Grandmother lived, my mother lived and I was born and able to build the time machine, travelled back in time, accidentally killed my Grandmother, wasn't born after all, etc.

How can one solve this paradox? Physicists solve it this way: The moment I accidentally killed my Grandmother, two parallel timelines emerge. One timeline in which I was born, another in which I wasn't born.

That's the theoretical basis of the "Parallel Worlds" Theory.

Proponents of this idea assume that there are many worlds that exist at the same time. I've created this exercise, so that you might experience a sense of parallel universes.

Remember a specific real situation from the past. The basis of this exercise is something that really happened. Dwell on that past scene for a few moments.

Notice how you made a decision back then, to go in a certain direction, to do a certain thing or to not do something.

Now imagine you'd have decided and acted differently. How would the events presumably develop on that parallel timeline? Speculate. Follow the track of this timeline as realistically as you possibly can.

Example:

1. You remember that a few months ago you were at a bus stop and had to decide whether to visit your girlfriend or go back home.
2. Back then you actually decided to go back home.
3. Imagine that you decided to go visit her. You enter the Bus and follow the events from that point forward. You have just entered a parallel timeline. Act as if this other version of you really does exist in a parallel world.

This does require some concentration, but it can be *very rewarding* and provide useful insights into life itself, alternative world and the *decisions* that create your reality. It can also provide surprising insights into which decisions you might take *next* that could improve your life.

Memories of the Future

And here is one final "time travel warm up exercise".

You are already used to remembering the so called past. You do it every day. Both past and future are things that are in your mind in the now. There actually is no past or future, only your thought about it. If you can therefore remember your past, you should also be able to remember your future. That's the exercise…to once in a while remember the future, not just the past. Simply act as if the future is already the past and "remember" it.

You might, for example remember things from the past…a love affair, a war, a fashion trend, music, a job, world events…and then "remember" the same thing in a future variation. Or you might occupy the viewpoint that you are currently in the year 2150 and remember what happened in the last 50 years.

We differentiate between "Memory" and "Imagination", but how exactly are these different? Have you ever, in your life, examined the difference closely? Have you ever taken the time to check: Do memory and imagination take place in different parts of the brain? Or are they not in the head at all, but rather in front of the forehead? Or is memory behind the head and imagination in front of it? Does memory feel different than imagination? If yes, how so?

Isn't it weird how many people spend an entire life without examining such basics?

Both memory and imagination are mind-pictures, are they not? "Memories" are supposedly images of things we have experienced and "Imagination" supposedly images of things we have not experienced. Or should we say "Not experienced YET"? Is Imagination a "Memory of the Future" or at the very least, a *possible* future? It's certainly food for thought.

4

Experience Reports

The most beautiful thing we can experience is the mysterious. It is the source of all true art and science. He to whom the emotion is a stranger, who can no longer pause to wonder and stand wrapped in awe, is as good as dead; his eyes are closed. – Albert Einstein

Every year, millions of people disappear from the face of the Earth. That's a statistical fact. Where do they disappear to? Some of the cases are due to crime. In some cases, people disappear to start a new life. And most cases actually remain *unexplained*. That's Millions of disappearances, worldwide, unexplained. And the real number is more in the range of tens of Millions.

There is no shortage of reports that people have unintentionally or intentionally stepped through time portals or have had time slips and…

…disappear forever (a guy walks around the corner and was never seen again)

…disappear and reappear (a guy walks around the corner, disappeared for many years. Recently he reappeared)

…show up from past or future (a guy nobody has seen before, shows up and claims to come from another time).

Throughout hundreds of years, many thousands of time travel reports have been collected and re-told. In the 20th Century these reports were published to a wider audience by authors such as John Keel, Charles Berlitz and Charles Fort. Not only have humans disappeared or appeared from nowhere, entire buildings and even cities have been reported to appear and disappear. In the 21st of Century, time slip stories come from regular people posting on the Internet.

The following are a few famous and well documented cases that convinced researchers and journalists of the reality of these events. I have also added cases from my own life as well as cases of people I have talked to personally that were able to convince me of their time travel. I have not included several thousand cases around "The Bermuda Triangle" or various alleged "Time Portals" around the world, which you can read up on elsewhere. This chapter is merely to provide a few tangible *examples* for your inspiration, not to provide an Encyclopedia of events.

A Versailles "Ghost Story"

This is a very well-known story, but I include it hear because it's important to know that not all apparitions are actually Ghosts or disembodied entities.

In the year 1911 two English Academics, Charlotte Moberly and Eleanor Jourdain published the book "An Adventure", in which they reported taking a trip through time, into the year 1780. The story was thought to be credible because of the impeccable reputation of these two women, who were the directors of St. Hughs College in Oxford. Further credibility was lent through the verifiability of all of their claims, the confirming reporting of two different Sources and the decades long, meticulous research into their story.

On August the 10th 1901, the two ladies decided to visit the Castle and Park of Versailles in France. Having viewed the impressive interior of the Castle, they walked through the Park in the direction of the "Petit Trianon", a House built in 1762 for the Mistress of King Louix XV. It was later used by Marie Antoinette, the last Queen of France before the Revolution.

Moberly and Jourdain

Somewhere around there, they lost their way. Within this time frame, they had the feeling that the atmosphere and landscape had changed – "the light no longer made shadows, there was no more wind and the leaves hung from their branches without moving" they wrote.

They did not see any other tourists far and wide. A short time later, they met two men who, in their old-fashioned outfits, looked like Gardeners. Asking them for the way, the men gave them a terse answer but kept following their walking path. Around this time Miss Moberly experienced a sudden onset of Sadness and Depression, as she later wrote in her Diary. She did not share this feeling with Mrs. Jourdain at the time. At the same time Miss Jourdain felt an overwhelming sense of Loneliness. But she also kept it from her companion. In the park they met several other people in what they thought was "time period" fashion. They seemed to notice the two ladies, but not perceive them clearly, as if they were Ghosts. The strange silence of the scene and the odd look of the people scared the ladies. They finally found the Petit Trianon House and saw a beautiful blond-haired woman wearing an old-fashioned hooped skirt, sitting on a chair in the grass, working with a drawing board. That is, Miss Moberly saw the women, Miss Jourdain did not see her, as they later realized. Miss Jourdain remembered a feeling of the "presence" of someone but did not see anyone. Soon they entered the Mansion and mingled with the tourists that were all dressed in modern clothing. They had arrived back in their time.

A few weeks had passed before Miss Moberly finally asked her companion: "Eleanor. Do you think that place was haunted?" She simply answered with "Yes, I believe so". It was only then that they began unraveling their story and comparing experiences. They came to the conclusion that they had experienced something very unusual: They had seen people from around 1780, shortly before the Revolution.

In the years that followed, both ladies visited Versailles several times, independently of each other. They both found that the atmosphere and landscape differed quite a lot from their first visit. Some buildings had disappeared, were the blonde woman was drawing there were now Bushes, brick walls blocked paths that they had walked on. Comprehensive research of the original floor plan and layout of the place and the fashion of the time let them believe that they really had traveled 120 years into the past. As much as the idea scared them, they stood their ground while the world, the experts and parapsychologists discussed the case. Some tried to find natural explanations, such as a costume festival taking place at the time. The claim was scrutinized and it was found that there was no costume festival on that date. Other claims were made and dismissed.

This is one of the best documented reports of a time jump, but there are many *thousands* of other well-known and similar reports. Some people say that there are time portals one can walk through. Some con-artists write books claiming they have "surefire methods to time travel" and then merely say "just find a time portal like they did in Versailles". But where are these time portals? And if they work, where will they take me? And how do I get back into my time? There are many idiotic books out there who not only don't answer such questions, they don't even ask them. The existence of a lot of bad books on time travel is what prompted me to write this one and I hope to be better. Sometimes I think really bad information is put out not to make money or entertain but to cover-up the real thing.

I do believe that time portals may open and close according to place, time and circumstance. What we know about Versailles and the Petit Trianon at the time prior to the French Revolution, is that it was a spiritually dark place. The mood of those days and the festering despair of the people, would eventually lead to one of the most bloody and murderous periods in Human History. That's why, in my view, Miss Moberly and Miss Jourdain felt such despair and loneliness when they travelled there. Compared to the "vibe" and "energy" of 1901, the atmosphere of France in 1780 was dense and sad. This told me that their story is likely valid, because it's precisely what the whole country must have *felt* like prior to the Revolution.

I don't believe that the location "Petit Trianon" has a fixed time portal. If that were so, you'd have heard reports from other tourists to Versailles. Unless of course, the ladies discovered a secret already existing portal by pure accident. Or perhaps time portals are benefited by extreme shifts in mood, emotion or atmosphere, such as was the case right before the French Revolution. Another possibility is that the "field" is messed up around Versailles because it's been the target of many time travelling tourists. The explanation that I favor, however, is that time portals are linked to a person's own consciousness. This is like in fairy tales where the magical device will only work with the right person. The magic wand, crystal or time portal won't work with the wrong person. I'd say the ladies were the right people, at the right time, in the right state of mind to have that experience and come back to report about it.

And yes, not all Ghosts are Ghosts. Some are apparitions from another time. I recall an incident where I saw apparitions playing soccer. I had first heard them play soccer somewhere behind the House where I was staying. When I went to investigate, I saw that the field from which I had heard the noise, was empty. There was nobody there. Then I heard the soccer ball being kicked and kids laughing again at night. I again went there and saw vague outlines of children and a ball. Then it disappeared and went quiet. The first time I saw this, I was frozen in terror. That's because I was not understanding what was being seen. But it happened a few more times over the weeks and I finally dared to just view it without fear. That's when I realized this was like a broken record, repeating certain events from another time. If I focused a little longer, I would have probably been able to enter a time portal right there and then. But back then I didn't know to. It appeared to me like there was a rift or cut in the fabric of reality. Imagine reality as a blanket. You tear a hole into it, and something else leaks through. I could imagine there is a way to mend these glitches in the matrix, but that particular one hadn't been fixed, so it kept playing the same scene. Maybe it was broken because something horrifying or wonderful had happened there. The emotional charge is still stored. This is essentially true of any place where very bad or very good things have happened: We feel that when we enter the place.

Time Travel in the Woods

At a younger age, I actually went looking for time portals or places where time anomalies had been reported. In my twenties, I'd read about some time anomaly get in my car and go there. These trips resulted in nothing. Well, not nothing. I always got to know great people and learned of new places. It then occurred to me that I didn't have to find other peoples' time portals, I could find my own, through intuition (see my two books on Intuition for more on that).

On the morning of the 6th of August 2002, I meditated for one hour on the intention of finding a time portal. I did so because I was writing the first version of this book. I was in the mood for it as I was staying overnight in a Hotel, outside of ordinary surroundings, and I did not have a computer with me to distract me (sophisticated smartphones were not yet public in those days). I focused on the feeling that it "were already true", as if I had already found that mysterious place. Around noon I went into the woods. This was in countryside Bavaria, Germany at the time. And even though I did not live far away, I was still staying in a Hotel as not to have to drive an hour home every day. I had a Seminar to conduct in that Hotel (yes, even back then I was conducting one Seminar or another). The woods were called "Ebersberger Forst" and is the largest *curated* forest in Europe. My intention to find a time portal was so firm that I actually took it as a given.

In retrospect, I suspect that me being near a time portal is what gave rise to the Intention. The Intention was inspired by the location. I began walking by intuition, not knowing exactly where. I didn't care how long I'd walk or how long it would take. I trusted I would experience something around time travel. I must have walked quite a long way because the sun was setting and I had begun my walk around midday. I worse no proper hiking shoes, just sneakers and felt blistering skin and ankle pain. It seemed like nothing had happened, except that I found a wallet a few hours back. I put the wallet into my pocket, intending to bring it back to its owner on another day. I had gotten lost a little and now tried to follow a footpath until it finally reached either a larger path or a street. When I finally got back to the Hotel it was almost Midnight and I went to bed pleasantly exhausted. On the next morning I realized I had not found the time portal I had hoped for. I checked myself. Did I not have the right intuition? Did I not follow it? Was my trust not adequate? I dropped the topic. But I dropped it too early as I was soon to find out.

A week later I finally got myself to try to return the wallet to its owner. Inside it there was a sticker with the owners address on it. How convenient.

You can imagine my surprise when I rang at the doorbell at that address and was told that a Person with that name does not live there. I showed the guy at the door the address sticker and the picture on the persons ID. He said: "Yeah, that might be the guy who lived here before us. But that was 7 years ago".

The wallet, picture and ID cards didn't look like they had been lying in the woods for 7 years. They looked as if they had been lost just hours before I found them. Upon closer inspection, the dates on the ID were that old and the credit cards had all expired! The whole episode put me in a kind of daze.

I arrived back home and wrote the event down. I felt euphoric. I had my time anomaly. I never found the owner of that wallet. And oddly enough, here in this year 2020, I don't even remember what I did with the wallet. I think I might have actually thrown it away. My one piece of evidence for time travel and I threw it away! Why? If I remember correctly, back then I suspected something bad had happened to the guy, otherwise he wouldn't have just left his wallet lying the forest. Not wanting a part in a potentially traffic event, I got rid of the wallet. I think that thought also cooled down my euphoria quite a bit.

The disappeared Laundromat

When the BBBC produced a TV Show about time anomalies in the 1980s, their studios were unexpectedly flooded with an avalanche of tens of thousands of letters that reported peoples' personal experiences with the same. People from all walks of society seemed to be time travelling!

One of the interesting accounts of time-shifting or "premonition" was of a teacher from the town of Halt in Norfolk, UK. One day he was stuck in a traffic jam and noticed that a laundromat that they had been building for some time, was finally finished and ready for use. Arriving home, he told his wife, who promptly took a basket of laundry and went there. Having arrived, she was surprised that the laundromat was not complete and construction workers were still working on it. It was opened six weeks later. The teacher had seen the finished laundromat in advance.

I share this particular story because it's one of the most common types of time-shifting. The stories of police officers, nurses, pilots, homeless, basketball players, clerks, kids, senior citizens, etc. about time-shifts would fill volumes. I have experienced them as well and described some of them in other books (particularly "Parallel Universes of Self").

Flight into the Future

In 1934 Victor Goddard, pilot of the British Royal Air Force, appears to have accidentally flown into the future.

He was flying from Andover England to Edinburgh. Above Scotland he came into a heavy storm and had to fly more deeply to detect landmarks or possibly make an emergency landing. He slowed his Hawker Hart airplane, reduced his altitude to find better weather below the clouds and to possibly find Drem, an airfield he assumed nearby. His intuition was correct. He saw Drem clearly visible in some distance. There he could land, refill and then continue his flight. A quarter mile from the airfield, something strange happened. The area was filled with an aetheric glow, as if the sun were shining on a summer day. Goddard saw the airfield full of life and activity. Mechanics in blue overalls were working on a number of yellow airplanes. He flew over it at a height of around 50 feet and all seemed well. But he found it odd that nobody was looking up at his airplane as he gained height and returned to the clouds. Because he was now clear about his location and direction, he decided to continue his flight without stopping.

A few days later Goddard looked into the Status of Drem airfield. He was shocked to find out that the airfield had been abandoned and was no longer in use for more than 10 years.

In the year 1938, Drem reopened as an Air Force School, due to the looming war. The color of British training aircraft changed from silver to yellow and uniforms changed from brown to blue. When Goddard visited the airfield in 1940, he noticed that it looked exactly like the one he had already seen in 1934. He had perceived what would happen 6 years in advance.

His story is popular and many of you might already know it, but I share it here because it shares commonalities with many other stories: A significant percentage of time travel stories come from pilots who have gone through thunderstorms. I'd say about 20% of the time travel stories I've read, are related to storms. Why do storms benefit openings in time? I don't know.

The Inventor of Movies on a Trip to Nowhere

The inventor of motion pictures, Louis Le Prince, had a promising future. On the 16th of September 1890 he presented his new invention at the Opera of Paris: Motion Pictures. It was the birth of Cinema and Movies. But exactly on this day, Le Prince got on a train in Paris and was never seen again. Both French authorities and British Detectives conducted intense investigations, without result.

Louis Le Prince, 1890

Thomas Edison finally collected the laurels for this invention. The Le Prince family went to Court against Thomas Edison, because he claimed to be the sole inventor of Cinema. The Le Prince family were also convinced that people linked to Edison had Le Prince killed, but a body was never found. Inexplicably, Edison won in Court and put the movie industry into his control for decades, similar to how Edison and the people behind him, took credit for the inventions of Nikola Tesla. At the time of his disappearance, Le Prince was about to patent his movie projector in the UK and then travel to the US for a scheduled New York exhibition. Some people claimed that he commit suicide due to "financial difficulties" but his widow not only denied such difficulties but also strongly denied that he would commit suicide at the peak of his success.

Seven year later Louis Augustin Le Prince was declared dead. The story is fairly well documented.

What is less known is that Le Prince had been talking about time travel to his family. He had told his sister that he was able to travel to the future and bring ideas for technology back into this time.

Considering he was *the first* to introduce movies, the idea that he might have travelled to the future to get the idea doesn't seem quite that far-fetched. How do you come up with ideas for moving pictures in 1890, unless you have at least some sense of the future?

Perhaps he introduced the idea a little too early and was "removed" for his invention by people around Edison, who preferred to have a monopoly on technology. Edison is widely considered the greatest inventor of all time, but I suspect he might be the greatest fraud of all time.

I share this story because it's in a class of its own, namely that of "inventor claiming to get ideas from the future". If you look into inventors a little, you'll find that many have made the claim that they somehow have access to the future from which they derive their ideas. Anyone with at least some intuitive feel for the future will be able to predict trends and tendencies far in advance.

The Hotel from Nowhere

The following story originates from the old British TV Show "Arthur C Clarkes World of Strange Powers". The show was respectable in that it used its own researchers to vet stories and claims of the paranormal.

The story comes from two couples from Dover, England that had apparently spent a night a Hotel from the past. In 1984 the story was once again newly researched and re-enacted for an Episode of the TV Series. The reason it was widely considered as 'probably true' is because of various congruencies found in the aftermath of the story.

In October 1979, Len and Cynthia Gisby and their friends Geoff and Pauline Simpson decided to travel to France. The took a Ferry over the English Channel to drive through France and Northern Spain for two weeks.

On the 3rd of October at around 9:30 pm they were on a highway north of Montelimar in Southern France. They had spent a pleasant day and were growing tired. It had gotten dark and was time to find a place to stay for the night. They stopped at a nice-looking Motel. Len went to the reception first to inquire about free rooms. Len reported that the Man was wearing a "somewhat strange plum colored uniform". The receptionist told them no rooms were available. He recommended another Hotel and told them to drive down the highway and another road, assuring that they would have rooms available. Len thanked him and the couples drove away. On the way Cynthia noticed how old the buildings looked. The posters that were glued to houses were advertising for a circus. "It seemed to be a really old-fashioned circus" Pauline later said. "That's why it fascinated us so much". The Men noticed the street that started showing a lot of potholes and unevenness and became very narrow. After a while they noticed that there was no more traffic and they started wondering whether their plan was all that good. But in some distance, they saw lights and drove on.

They stopped at a building right at the street. It was a deep, long building with a number of bright windows. A few men stood in front of it. Cynthia got out, but soon came back to the car. "That's not a Hotel, it's a Restaurant".

They continued their drive through an Avenue of Trees on both sides of a dark road and soon reached other buildings. One of them seemed to be a police station. The other said "Hotel". Relieved that their trip seemed to be over, Len got out and asked the reception for accommodation. He returned to the car thankful. "They do have rooms". The tired drivers unpacked their bags while wondering about the old fashioned, farm like style of the Hotel. They entered the Hotel and there too found farm-like conditions. The building had two floors. Neither the Simpsons nor the Gisbys spoke French and the Receptionist or Manager apparently spoke no English. The communication was just barely enough to show them their rooms. The strange atmosphere continued all the way to their rooms. Everything was old and made of heavy wood. There were no table cloths on the dining room tables and there did not seem to be any phones or any other modern gadgets.

The rooms in the bed were big, but they had no pillows, only cushion pads. The blankets were heavy and the mattresses sacked down in the middle. The doors had no locks, they had wooden bolts. The couples had to share a bathroom with old fashioned toilet drainage and soap that was attached to a metal bar in the wall. But they were too tired to wonder about it, went to bed and slept through the night.

The next morning, they went down to the dining room for breakfast. The breakfast was quite simple: Bread, Marmalade and Coffee. Geoff remembered that the Coffee tasted horrible. While they had breakfast, another woman entered the dining room and sat down somewhere across from them. She wore a silk evening gown and carried a dog in her arm. "It was so strange" Pauline remembers. "She looked as if she had just come from a dancing ball, but it was 7 in the morning".

Then two policemen in dark blue uniforms, capes and big pointed hats arrived. "They looked ridiculous. Much different than the policemen that we saw elsewhere in France" remembered Geoff. "Their uniforms were also old fashioned". Len and Geoff wanted to ask the policemen for the best way to Avignon by "Autoroute" (Highway), but the officers didn't understand the word "Autoroute". At the time Geoff assumed it was because of his poor French. Before they left the Hotel, they shot a few Photos. Geoff took pictures of Pauline at the framed windows. Len took two Photos of Cynthia.

They stowed their stuff in the car and Len went to the Manager asking for the invoice. The man scribbled the amount on a piece of paper and showed him the Bill which came to the amazingly small sum of 19 Francs (a value of about $3 Dollars). Len tried to explain to the Receptionist that the price was too low, but he insisted that the price was correct. He paid and they left the Hotel.

The rest of their vacation was uneventful. They went to Spain. On their way back to England, through France, they decided to stop at the same Hotel they had been to because they were flabbergasted by its low price. They found the exit and they also saw the strange Circus Posters again, so they knew they were on the right way.

But they couldn't find the Hotel. They were worried enough to drive back to the Motel on the Highway and ask for the way to that Hotel. But the receptionist had no idea of any Hotel in the area. Not only that, he also denied the existence of a colleague in a plum colored uniform. The two couples drove up and down the street four times, but they found no Hotel. It had disappeared. They noted that the area looked very similar to the one they had been to a few days before but also that it "somehow looked different" even though they couldn't define what exactly was different. Puzzled, they continued their journey until they arrived in Lyon, where they spent a night in a Hostel for 247 Francs (around $40).

After their trip, the mystery deepened when they looked at their freshly developed photographs. Geoff had taken 20 pictures and Len had taken 36. The Photos in the Hotel were supposed to be in between the others. But they were missing. Nor were there any corrupted negatives. Every film was fully used, as if the pictures had never been made. They had disappeared, just like the Hotel.

During the filming of the TV Show, the Simpsons and Gisbys were flown back to France to film their search of the Hotel. Geoff Simpson: "When we went back, we had yet another look around. Once we even thought we might have found the Hotel. But it wasn't our Hotel, just some old House that was completely different. At the place where we all agreed and were sure that our Hotel stood, there was nothing". The French Tourist Information Office in Lyon said that there was no Hotel as the one the Simpsons and Gisbys described.

In July 1985 Journalist and Paranormal Researcher Jenny Randles, accompanied by her colleagues Linda Taylor and Harry Harris spent an evening with the Simpsons. After the interview, they were scheduled to go to the practice of Dr. Albert Keller for Hypnosis Session, to be regressed back to that day. Pauline was unable to be hypnotized, but Geoff turned out to be a good subject. He gave a detailed description of the event, but no new Elements were discovered. The Hypnosis session did confirm that Geoff was remembering an event that actually happened.

A question that remained unanswered was: Why did the manager and the other people "from the past" not notice the car that must have looked futuristic? Why did the receptionist not notice that the money they paid with was from 1979?

And my most important question is: Why was there no research into whether there was a Hotel at that place in another time? That bothers me the most about so many of these "Paranormal Mystery" TV Shows. They are strong in sensationalism and marketing but weak in research and thoroughly unsatisfying in the pursuit of truth.

The reason I share this story anyway is because time slips are real. I have experienced a few of them personally, so I am more than willing to believe in others experience. In fact, I probably wouldn't bother writing this book if I hadn't had my own experiences in time travel.

I also share it, because there is a specific reason the people in the past did not see the car, the future-money or the cameras, which I'll explain soon.

Spinning to Another Time

I had one of my most intense personal time slips on the Island of Malta. And Malta is what I'd consider a really weird

Island, I can't make much sense of it. Its official language is English, even though it's nowhere near other English-speaking countries but just north of Libya and South of Sicily. It has the cars and buses of London as well as the left side driving, but the people look like a mix of Arabic and Sicilian. But their original language is related neither to Italian nor Arabic but is a (to my ears) exotic sounding tongue full of x and ch sounds. From my stays and experiences there, the Island also appears to be remarkably corrupt. In addition to all of that, it is also ridiculously small, almost too small to be its own country. I can drive to one point of the country to another in half an hour.

In my early twenties I conducted English and NLP-Courses there, in large and beautiful 5-star Hotels, on behalf of the Trainings Institute that sent me there. One evening, I was listening to a recording that claimed to deliver extra-low-frequency-waves behind a background of white noise. I was supposed to listen to it for one hour in order to synchronize the hemispheres of my brain. But I had fallen asleep while listening and had the audio-player on auto-repeat. After many hours of the white noise coming through the headphones I was in a peculiar state between waking and sleeping and got the strangest sensation: That of my mind or energy rotating...quicker and quicker and quicker. The rotation continuously sped up and was accompanied by a high-pitched tone. I had the feeling of leaving my body or of not being properly attached it in the first place, as if oscillating between body and out-of-body. I removed the headphones, turned off the audio-player and re-oriented myself in the hotel room. It was a sunny day outside. This was confusing, because I had started my exercise at 10 p.m. when it was already dark. Had I really slept all night? I felt disoriented and spaced-out and went to take a shower in order to get grounded. Back then I did not wear a wrist-watch, but the alarm-clock in the bedroom showed 3:00 o'clock. My expectation was that this should be 3 a.m. but it must have been 3 p.m. because it was sunny and hot daylight outside.

I went to the reception desk to verify the time. Indeed, it was 3 in the afternoon. I could not understand how I slept all night and a large part of the next day without noticing. As far as I was concerned, I was only dozing two hours or so. And I did not believe that my earphones could have remained on my ears for 17 hours straight…or that my nearly used up batteries last that long. Confusion welled up in my mind. I stepped outside into a temperature way above the comfort zone I was accustomed to. The thermometer read 40 degrees Celsius. I walked around in a daze, gradually trying to accept that I had slept 17 hours straight. It then suddenly hit me that I must have missed an appointment for lunch that day. I had gotten to know a French woman a few days before and had arranged to meet her for lunch today! So, I phoned her apologizing for missing the date. But she responded in her French accent: "oh no, no, no, no. It's ok. Our meeting is tomorrow!" Tomorrow? I accepted the schedule, thinking I had misunderstood our dates timing.

Later in the day, while reading the days newspaper to a cup of coffee, I had a realization in the classical sense of a character in a science-fiction movie. I was reading the same newspaper I had read "yesterday". Asking the waiter if they had today's newspaper, he told me I am holding today's newspaper and that they throw away newspapers from previous days. I looked at the day, and it was Tuesday, although in my mind it was supposed to be Wednesday. As far as I was concerned, I had started my Extra-Low-Frequency-Meditation on Tuesday at 10 p.m. Now I was sitting here and it was Tuesday all over again! Had I time-travelled? Had I actually really time-travelled? Had my childhoods dream come true without me even being fully aware let alone appreciative of it? I racked by brains for other explanations. Maybe it had been Monday and I only thought it was Tuesday. It was my mistake for sure. But feeling more and more confused I had to know for certain. I retraced my days. "Sunday I definitely remember because all the shops were closed and I had to drink out of the mini-bar of the Hotel. And it was on Sunday that I told myself I would go Paragliding above the Ocean (called Parasailing). And it was on Sunday I looked up various offers on Parasailing. And it was on Monday I actually went Parasailing. I know it was Monday because that's when I went Parasailing and all the shops were open again. I went with a friend of mine who was shaking with fear of heights while acting as if everything was OK. Yes, that was Monday. It was Monday because it felt unique to not begin a working week on Monday but rather continue leisurely island life (I had done a Seminar on Malta the Week before). I traced Monday into the evening. I recall spending time at the beach with my French acquaintance. That's when we arranged to meet on Wednesday for lunch. That's also when I decided that I would do Meditation on Tuesday evening, the evening spent without her. There was no meditation Monday evening. I was with her. I woke up on Tuesday and spent much of the time idly hanging around at the Hotel Pool, reading. Later I retreat to my room to do some writing on my laptop. And then at around 10 p.m. I started using the Audio-Program to meditate. I recall falling asleep after about 40 Minutes of it. And then waking up…to daylight…not on Wednesday but on Tuesday. There was now no doubt in my mind that I had time-travelled. So…being on Tuesday again…shouldn't I be seeing the other Version of myself on that day? But I didn't. That other Tuesday was apparently taking place in a parallel universe. I spent the rest of the day in a silent joy over the accomplishment of time-travel.

The shop that transformed into something else

The following is quoted from the book "Secret Liverpool "by Mark and Michelle Rosney, 2015.

Bold Street in Liverpool has been associated with time slips for decades, with many people having testified that this bustling, shop-lined high street contains a passageway to the past.

One of the earliest known accounts is said to date back to 1996, when Frank, a police officer from Merseyside, went shopping with his wife, Carol. It was a sunny, Saturday afternoon and the pair agreed to split up: Frank wanted to look for a new CD at a music shop, and Carol wanted to go to Dillon's Bookshop on Bold Street. Frank agreed to meet his wife at the bookshop, and so, after finishing at the music shop, walked into Bold Street. Upon passing The Lyceum, a nineteenth-century neoclassical building which marks the entrance of the road, Frank claimed to have felt a peculiar sensation. Everything had gone quiet.

Before he had a chance to ponder this change any further, a small box van supposedly honked its horn and skidded around Frank, narrowly missing him. The police officer claimed that the van looked as though it belonged in the 1950s, and had the name "Caplan's" (or "Caplin's", depending on the variant of the story) stenciled on its side. Confused, Frank stepped out of the road and headed in the direction of Dillon's Bookshop. As he got closer, however, he saw that the name "Cripps" hung above the shop, and that rather than displaying books, the windows were lined with women's handbags and shoes.

According to the police officer's story, it was then that he looked around and realised that people in the street were dressed rather strangely, seemingly wearing clothing from the 1940s and 50s. One person, a young woman in her twenties, stood out from the rest: she was dressed in a lime-coloured sleeveless top, and carried a handbag that Frank recognised as a popular modern-day brand. They smiled at each other as she passed him and headed into Cripps. As he followed her inside, it is claimed that the interior of the shop suddenly changed. Gone were the handbags and shoes, and in their place were bookshelves laden with paperbacks. Frank turned to the young woman, who seemed to be equally confused. When he asked her if she had seen what he had, she supposedly said yes and explained that she had thought it was a new clothes shop, and had been surprised to find the building full of books. Befuddled, Frank found his wife and went home, unable to shake his experience.

Later, he found out that a local business called Caplan's did once exist, and that the bookshop he agreed to meet his wife in used to be a ladies' shawl shop called Cripps.

The reason I added this well-known story (and Bold Street in Liverpool has dozens), is because it shows that time-slips are often a matter of fading in and out. My time slip in Malta was not of this type. As far as I know, I never returned to my original timeline. Luckily, I only travelled back by half a day. But in general, people tend to fade in and out of the time naturally and easily, as if there is a corrective force that knows to which time they belong.

People in past times do not seem to recognize or only vaguely recognize discrepancies and oddities in the time travelers' fashion or their machinery. I believe this is due to how human *perception* works – we have difficulty actually seeing something we do not know or believe. The nature of reality itself is fluid enough to adapt to our beliefs. So, the hotel receptionist from the past, would have seen contemporary coins, so formed by his own beliefs or would not have noticed the cars, similar to how the native tribes of some places could not see Christopher Columbus gigantic ships because they didn't believe such existed. Some people in the past, can see though, and react with shock, amusement or curiosity. These are probably people who are less stubborn or rigid in their way of thinking, open minded enough to consider anything. It is also interesting that many time-slip experiencers were unable to take objects with them to their native time. Pictures taken there, objects taken with them, seemed to disappear on their return. That's one of the reasons I say that Time Travel is more strongly linked to Consciousness and Perception than to a physical activity. Time travel is a radical shift in Consciousness. People were able to perceive and to some extent interact with other times. But they were unable to transpose objects from one time in to another. Had they been able to do so, it would probably not be a matter of fading in and out, but rather difficult to return to one's original time.

Very Old Envelope

Having just explained the general rule that no physical evidence is transported back from timeslips, here is an exception.

It pertains to a Mr. Squirrel, who entered a Pharmacy in 1973 in the English town of Yarmouth. He was there to purchase envelopes. He was served by a lady who wore clothing from the long-gone Victorian era. He bought three envelopes. He also noticed that it was extremely quiet in the shop. The usual street noise had disappeared.

When he visited the shop again three weeks later, it seemed to have completely changed and modernized. The clerk, an older lady, insisted that the Shop hadn't changed compared to the week before. And she also assured him that no other clerk would have been present a week ago.

The envelopes fell apart after a short time (even though it is possible, it doesn't seem to be easy to take objects from other timelines. The disintegration of objects from other rimes is a common theme in time-travel stories). Paranormal Author Joan Forman heard of the incident and interviewed Mr. Squirrel. He was able to show her one of the envelopes that was still somewhat intact. Joan Forman wrote to the producer of the envelopes and was told that they no longer produce the envelopes for 15 years.

What is unclear to me in this story is whether Mr. Squirrel was oscillating between two different pasts...one of the Victorian Era and one of envelopes that were 15 years old, or whether the envelopes had been produced for hundreds of years.

Why do objects from other times seem to disappear or quickly disintegrate or "go lost"? I suspect there are laws in the universe that protect the stability and integrity of various timelines and realities. If substance A is not native to Reality B, it will not stay there long, just like the vegetable oil in my pan will not stay with the water. It's a matter of two different vibrations not being compatible.

Audience from the Past

Vera Conway arrived in a London building for a music lesson. She went to the first floor; mistaking directions, she entered a door between the two cloakrooms. This door led directly to the past. She found herself in a theatre, but realized that the audience was in period dress, possibly from the Regency period. A man approached her wearing breeches and powdered hair. There were no electric lights, just lanterns. Vera felt strangely out of place, but no one appeared to notice anything amiss about her. It was almost as if the audience had expected her. Realizing something was wrong, she left the theater and returned to the reception to again ask for directions. She later returned to that corridor and determined for certain that there was no door between the two cloakroom doors.

I include this well-known story, first published in 1995, because it again shows how time travelers often blend in to the expectations of people in the past, without seeming out of place. This again supports my theory that much of what we perceive is created by Consciousness and time travel is primarily a matter of consciousness. If there are time machines, they do not work independently of the user's consciousness.

Parallel San Francisco

Around 20 years ago, an acquaintance of mine reported of intense Dreams that she had that took her to a parallel world version of her hometown San Francisco. While she lived there, she had a Phase of about four weeks where she had dreams of different Versions of her city almost every night. I first wrote about these in my 2001 book "Time Travel".

One of the versions horrified her. The infrastructure was run down, stray cats, wild dogs and rats were festering through the streets and so she went back home quickly to look at the city from the safety of her window. The city was in a state of decay. In the distance she saw explosions. San Francisco wasn't doing too well.

In another dream she was again walking in the city, but apparently the one she knew. She wasn't aware that she was dreaming and decided to go shopping. The problem arose when a shop clerk didn't want to accept her credit card. She asks "Why are you giving me this?" – "To pay" she said "Is this some kind of joke?" the clerk responded. As she only had her credit card with her, she stepped away from the cash desk and watched other people paying. Others paid either in cash or put their thumbs on a glass surface. Their thumbprints were scanned and that apparently passed as payment. In that moment she became lucid and realized she was dreaming again. Rather than having travelled to some kind of future, she had again slipped into a parallel timeline in which credit cards were apparently never created. Inspired to find out other small differences, she went for a walk. Everything seemed to be as she knew. The interesting thing about this dream is that it was without distortion, dream-weirdness or sudden shifts in place. It was a very unusual dream as the place was stable and the people appeared to be real. She was lucid enough to go look for indicators that she was in a parallel version of that city. On a screen in some shop she saw the President speaking, but it was no President that she knew. The Date was also visible at the bottom of the screen: 23rd of July 1999, which matched the time she was having the dream. It's rare that specific numbers can be read in dreams, which is a testimony to how intense it was.

She had another five experiences in parallel universes. In one of them culture, technology and economic success had beautifully merged. The buildings were creatively built and colored, there was lots of green. She recognized a few buildings, but most of them were built round, not square. The people in this variation looked satisfied.

Abbeville Louisiana Time Travel

This story is taken from Strange Magazine, Issue 2, Spring 1988.

I take pleasure in sharing with you the following occurrence because I personally interviewed one of the parties involved, and have repeatedly gone over the incident with him these past six years. L.C. (his real initials) has been my friend for fifteen years, but as we visited together one day about six years ago, he told me of this most amazing event in his life which haunts him to this day.

L.C. and a business associate, Charlie, (fictitious name) had just finished lunch in the small Southwest Louisiana town of Abbeville. Still discussing their work, they began their drive north along Highway 167 towards the Oil Center city of Lafayette about 15 miles away. The date was October 20, 1969, and the time was about 1:30 in the afternoon. It was one of those picture-perfect days in Fall--clear blue skies and a nippy 60 degrees, just right conditions for cruising along with the car windows rolled down.

The highway had been practically traffic-free until they spotted some distance ahead what appeared to be an old turtle-back-type auto traveling very slowly. As they closed the distance between their vehicle and this relic from the past, their discussion turned from their insurance work to the old car ahead of them. While the style of the auto indicated it to be decades old, it appeared to be in show room condition, which evoked words of admiration from both L.C. and Charlie. Because the car was traveling so slowly, the two men decided to pass it, but before doing so, slowed to better appreciate the beauty and mint condition of the vehicle. As they did so, L.C. noticed a very large bright orange license plate with the year "1940" clearly printed on it. This was most unusual and probably illegal unless provisions had been made for the antique car to be used in ceremonial parades.

As they passed the car slowly to its left, L.C., who was in the passenger's seat, noticed the driver of the car was a young woman dressed in what appeared to be 1940 vintage clothing. This was 1969 and a young woman wearing a hat complete with a long colored feather and a fur coat was, to say the least, a bit unusual. A small child stood on the seat next to her, possibly a little girl. The gender of the child was hard to determine as it too wore a heavy coat and cap. The windows of her car were rolled up, a fact which puzzled L.C. because, though the temperature was nippy, it was quite pleasant and a light sweater was sufficient to keep you comfortable. As they pulled up next to the car, their study turned to alarm as their attention was riveted to the animated expressions of fear and panic on the woman's face. Driving alongside of her at a near crawl (no traffic in either direction allowed this maneuvering) they could see her frantically looking back and forth as if lost or in need of help. She appeared on the verge of tears.

Being on the passenger's side, L.C. called out to her and asked if she needed help. To this she nodded "yes," all the while looking down (old cars sat a little higher than the low profiles of today's cars) with a very puzzled look at their vehicle. L.C. motioned to her to pull over and park on the side of the road. He had to repeat the request several times with hand signs and mouthing the words because her window was rolled up and it seemed she had difficulty hearing them. They saw her begin to pull over so they continued to pass her so as to safely pull over also in front of her. As they came to a halt on the shoulder of the road, L.C. and Charlie turned to look at the old car behind them. However, to their astonishment, there was no sign of the car. Remember, this was on an open highway with no side roads nearby, no place to hide a car. It and its occupants had simply vanished.

L.C. and Charlie looked back at the empty highway. As they sat in the car, spellbound and bewildered, it was obvious to them that a search would prove futile. Meanwhile, the driver of a vehicle that had been behind the old car pulled over behind them. He ran to L.C. and Charlie and frantically demanded an explanation as to what had become of the car ahead of him. His account was as follows. He was driving North on Highway 167 when he saw, some distance away, a new car passing up a very old car at a slow pace, so slow that they appeared to be nearly stopped. He saw the new car pull onto the shoulder and the old car started to do the same. Momentarily, it obstructed the new car and then suddenly disappeared. All that remained ahead of him was the new car on the shoulder of the highway. Desperate to associate logic to this incredible sight, he immediately assumed an accident had occurred. Indeed, an accident had not occurred, but something more haunting, perhaps as tragic, and certainly more mysterious had.

After discussing what each had seen from his perspective, the three men walked the area for an hour. The third man, who was from out of state, insisted on reporting the incident to the police. He felt that it was a "missing person" situation and that they had been witnesses. L.C. and Charlie refused to do so as they had no idea where the woman and child along with the car had gone. They were missing alright, but no police on this plane of existence had the power to find them. The third man finally decided that without their cooperation he could not report this on his own for fear his sanity would be questioned. He did exchange addresses and phone numbers with L.C. and Charlie. For years he kept in touch with them, calling just to talk about his incident and to confirm again that he had seen what he had.

I include this story because it is common for one to fade in and out of certain times rather than permanently manifest in one time only. Both the 1940s woman and the 1969 men faded in and out of each other's realities. She was likely seeing some of theirs as they were seeing some of hers. She was probably seeing more of theirs as she was in near panic, while the guys were fairly relaxed over what they thought was a lady going to some vintage show.

Dreams of Distant Future

I knew as a child who I would one day marry and which country we'd live in. I saw her in nightly recurring dreams. After a while, I forgot about her. I married in my early thirties, but not the woman I had seen in my childhood dream. I divorced in my late thirties. Shortly thereafter I got to know the woman I had seen such a long time ago. We ended up marrying shortly thereafter and also moving to that country predicted long ago.

Oddly enough, in the dreams, I saw us riding around in a flying car. But cars were not flying when I got to know her and are not flying today. Sometimes I have the strange premonition that cars were meant to be flying by the 2010s. We still got to know each other and still married and she looks exactly like I knew she would. I don't know if she grasps that I have known her since childhood. But the flying cars weren't there, as if we had entered an alternate, somewhat technologically "lesser" timeline. As I write these words, I can sense a version-of-me on another timeline that doesn't even write this paragraph, because in his world, cars fly.

New Zealand River Tip Head Has Anomalous Aura

The following story was submitted to a Blog that collects peoples personal time slip accounts. There are many private Blogs such as this, on the Internet. I got the story from here:

https://timeslipaccounts.blogspot.com/2009/

Almost five years ago [circa 1997] when I lived in Blaketown, a suburb of Greymouth, a town on the South Island of New Zealand, my friend and I were down at the "tip head." A tip head in New Zealand speak is a man-made bank that extends a river bank where it meets the sea. In the case of Blaketown, it's used to control the flow of the river.

I'm not entirely sure which of us came up with the bright idea to go on this night; it was very windy, the waves were big and breaking on the tip (not strong enough to wash us off though -- they rarely are) and the dark clouds suggested rain very soon. The tip has a ramp leading to a lower platform on the riverside where ships used to load and unload cargo. My friend was looking down at this platform when I noticed a very big wave approaching. I told him it was time to move but he didn't respond. Something seemed very wrong -- it's like he wasn't even there. He snapped out of it after I screamed at him a few times and we got out of the way. He was completely freaking out. I asked him why he didn't respond and he said he'd seen a vision of ship. It was daytime in this vision and lots of people were about, loading up this old-fashioned steam ship. It was an ordinary, simple scene, which discounts both a past life recollection (ones not prompted by hypnosis are nearly always the death of the life in question) and an atmospheric photograph ghost (assuming strong emotions are the key to such things).

We went back the next day and his description of the tip in his vision squared with what's there today to a T. He said the ramp had a cart on it, mounted on train rails. While there are no rails there today, there are further towards land and the concrete on the ramp is of a noticeably different grain to the rest of the platform. He said that the tip seemed shorter and, again, a different grain of concrete towards the end suggests this is true. He said that there were streams of water pouring off the sides of the tip, and there are remnants of wooden channels on the surface. These were obviously intended to siphon water from breaking waves off quicker. I asked him how he felt during the vision and he said, "I felt like I was there, but shouldn't have been." The people in this vision gave no indication they knew of his "presence," but this is hardly a relevant detail as it can't have lasted more than 10 seconds.

This person in question was and still is one of my best friends: an observant, intelligent and logical but still open-minded man who is currently in the Air Force. We'd been down to the tip at night a hundred times before and a hundred since and nothing like it has ever happened again.

The sea around the tiphead is very rough, and the entry to the river is very hazardous at times. Many ships have gone down in the area, and I'd be surprised if the place hasn't seen at least one suicide. There's a monument down there to the people who've drowned in the area over the years. It's got about a dozen plaques on it, and if anything it's underused. When I head down there at night, even when I think about all this stuff, it doesn't bug me. But some nights there's just...something about the place. One night it was a beautifully clear and calm night, New Year's about 1999 if I'm not mistaken. The view from the end would've been something special, but my friend (a different one) and I both agreed: Something wasn't right. Another time I was down there with the friend who had the timeslip; we got halfway down the road and I couldn't get away fast enough.

I've often wondered if the emotional imprint/atmospheric photograph-type ghosts aren't just timeslips manifesting to a weaker level. There are too many ghosts who obviously are not sentient but also aren't doing anything that would suggest a strong emotional situation is the trigger. You also have to factor in the surroundings -- some places haven't changed much over the years to the casual observer. Also, if the experience features people, then the person viewing the thing might be so caught up (e.g.: "Holy shit, there's a dude in a suit of armor!") in what's going on to really take in the fact that the scenery's changed as well. Basically, I think timeslips are probably more common than they at first appear.

I shared this as an example of a non-famous story of a regular internet poster. You can find many more on various private blogs and discussion boards.

The Woolwich Tunnel

This story was published on the website "Portals of London":

https://portalsoflondon.com/2017/07/02/the-woolwich-anomaly/

It was taken up by large newspapers, such as The Guardian.

When the Woolwich foot tunnel closed for repairs in 2011, it should have been a routine job. The pathway had been providing pedestrians with a quick route beneath the Thames since 1912. A century on, a few minor improvements were necessary. Contractors were hired to plug holes, improve access and bring communications capabilities into the 21st Century: swapping leaky tiles for a leaky feeder.

But Woolwich residents will recall that the refurb of this much loved and much used walkway did not go according to plan. When it finally re-opened it was 8 months behind schedule, having been closed for more than a year and a half. What the average Woolwich dweller doesn't know, however, are the unusual circumstances behind this delay.

Mention the 18 month time frame to someone who worked on the Woolwich Tunnel job and you may be met with a mysterious smile. A year and a half may have seemed a long time to those who relied on the tunnel for their daily commute. But for those who were down there beneath the river, that time-frame has a different meaning. When one contractor tells me he aged 3 years on the Woolwich job, it is not a metaphor. For, deep down beneath river and clay, hidden from those above ground, something was occurring. That something was a time anomaly.

A time anomaly, from the perspective of someone who experiences it, involves a clearly defined part of landscape or architecture, in which time 'stops'. Years of study into such phenomena has proved largely fruitless in terms of explanations.

And even less so when it comes to predicting when and where they might arise. There is some anecdotal evidence that temporary spaces, or spaces temporarily under a different use, lend themselves to time anomalies, and the Woolwich event would appear to support this.

But they are notoriously hard to define – not having experienced one, PoL isn't about to try. The best thing we can do is listen to those that have experienced them. The following testimony is from one of the contractors on the Woolwich foot tunnel job (he wishes to remain anonymous). His words are presented uninterrupted, with as little editing as possible.

"I was one of the first ones to experience it. We were working from both ends, as it were, and had tents on both sides of the river. It was pretty basic, if you wanted something from the other side, you just had to walk it through the tunnel. Anyway the foreman's on the other side and he radios to ask me across. So I walk through the tunnel – the 'long walk', we called it, funnily enough – and it's slightly spooky because no one else is down there, they're all working on the lift shafts, and I get up the other side, find the foreman, and his eyes nearly pop out of his head. Says he only radioed like a minute ago and how did I get there so quick? Wouldn't take my word for it I'd walked. Reckoned I had a buggy down there or something, that it was some kind of prank.

But I stand my ground and he starts to see I'm not lying. Anyway he forgets what he called me there for. He gives me this big red plastic box, tells me to walk back over and hold it up for him when I get to the other side. So I head back down, the lonely walk back, thinking shouldn't we be getting on with some work. When I get to the top I wave the red box in the air and radio the foreman. 'You just left me!' he's saying, 'No more than a minute ago'. That's when I start to feel a bit weird.

My initial feelings was I was pretty freaked out by it all. But once everyone else had experienced it, it was amazing how quickly it seemed normal. It became like a joke. It was a laugh, you know, a source of giggles. Someone said we'd invented the teleporter and were all going to be rich. The foreman stopped trusting watches and phones when we were down there, and took to using egg-timers. A few of the young agency lads tried to claim extra on their time sheets. That was the thing, though: time froze when you were down there. If you were down there for the full working day, fixing the tiling, you'd basically finish work, come back up and it would still be morning. Which was great at first – I don't live in London so I did a lot of sightseeing, Cutty Sark, The Royal Palaces – but then we all realised how knackered we were.

It never really occurred to any of us to tell anyone about it at the time. It was like, who would believe you? You didn't even believe it yourself. Plus it was such a wheeze. I think there was a feeling that as soon as head office was on to it the whole thing would be over. No more fun.

People started experimenting. Some of the guys camped out in there to see how long they could. 3 days and nights it was, and they still came back at the same moment they'd left. That freaked the site manager out though. He was having a nightmare with the timetables as it was. Biggest problem was making sure that if anyone from head office came down it wouldn't look like he was sending people home ten minutes after they logged on – although that's exactly what he was doing. Anyway he soon put a stop to all the mucking about.

Not before I had my one very strange moment, though.

One thing we couldn't get our head round was how the two, sort of, time-places a guy was in seemed to be happening at the same time, as it were. Like I see you emerge across the river in no time at all, but there's also a 'you' who reckons he's spending four hours in the tunnel.

So Petar, this Bulgarian lad, thought of a little experiment. One morning before anyone else is down the tunnel, he ties a long rope round his waist, and hands the other end to some of the guys. Then he sets off down the tunnel, see. And I'm to follow him down as far as the bottom of the stairs, and then stop and watch him walk down the tunnel. 'Don't put your foot off the stairs, don't step in the tunnel', he told me. And I didn't.

So I'm watching him, and he's got something in his pocket, a secret signal for when he's across the river, when he gets to the surface. When the others see he's surfaced, they're supposed to shout down at me and pull on the rope. Anyway, I'm kneeling down and craning my head down so I can watch Petar walk around the curve, [the tunnel bends in an inverted bow underground – PoL] and he laughs and waves at me for a minute, then gets bored, keeps walking. And he's just about to round the curve, out of sight – it hasn't been long, just a minute or so, around the same time it'd took us to walk down the steps – and I feel the rope around me tighten. Then I hear the lads up top. 'He's across. Waving a red flag'. The thing is, Petar hears it too.

And he stops. Turns round. And he's looking at me. His hand slowly reaches into his big jacket pocket, and he pulls out the edge of this large red flag. For a moment I grin. I reckon they're all having me on. But it's the look on his face, that's what still haunts me. Nobody's that good an actor. His face – and he's a big man, mind you, fearless. Our Petar was a big character, always at the centre of things, always with this big smile. Never saw him take anything too serious in all our days til then, but – I don't know how to describe it, it was – fear. Just plain fear on his face. And he's looking right at me and I know what he's thinking. I know what he's trying to figure out – do I keep going, or do I come back? He takes one step towards me, then stops. I don't know how long we looked at each other like that, neither of us talking. Then in the end he turns round again, and carries on, out of sight.

Well, I'm up those stairs like a shot and when I get up top there he is, across the river, unmistakeable even from that distance, red flag in one hand, another guy's arm around his shoulders.

Anyway I didn't like that. That freaked me out, that did. Petar didn't talk about it much. Nobody spoke much about any of it after that. The jokes kind of came to an end and we just got on with the job. Tried to ignore it."

The tunnel was re-opened in early 2012. No time-discrepancies have been reported since that date.

That completes the Experience Reports section. I could fill an entire book with these stories. In fact, I could fill a dozen books. I'm sure these were enough to get the gist of it.

The Meaning of Timeslips

The phenomena described in this chapter are so common, that we have many words to describe them:

Timeslip

Timewarp

Timeshift

Timejump

Time Dislocation

Temporal Displacement

Temporal Rift

Time Anomaly

Dimensional Shift

And more.

Timeslips usually refer to spontaneous or unintended Time Travel, a temporary distortion of the fabric of time that eventually self-corrects. Imagine someone bending a piece of rubber. When the person lets go, it automatically forms back into its original shape and everything is in the place it was before. It also seems that one can intentionally leave a scene, such as a shop, a garden or a space to return to one's native time. One could therefore say that certain time slips are temporarily linked to certain places. Maybe some doors open only at some places, at some times, for some people.

Timeslips are often accompanied by an odd distortion of perception that allows one to pay with 2020 money in the year 1932 for example. Skeptics say that these cases are proof that the stories are invented. With just a little more intelligence than the average "Skeptic" you realize that, if the story were invented, one could tell it, without inconsistencies. One could make something up to solve that problem. It's easy to make up stories. But if one were to make them up, why add items that arouse that much skepticism?

In my experience, people only see what they are willing to see and when time travelers from the future visit you, you may not even notice. There is some unknown law in the Universe that allows for paradoxical situations. The Universe will not allow entire timelines to be mixed up just because of a little glitch.

On the 10th of August 1901, one day before Miss Moberly and Miss Jourdain travelled through time, meteorologists recorded an intense electrical storm over Europe. The air on that day was filled with electricity. Might that have led to the temporary timeslip in Versailles?

Some researchers say that Timeslips are abilities of the people who experience them and that no other could experience that. Some parapsychologists say that the time-slipping person was at that exact place in another life and was now viewing it from the viewpoint of another self in another time.

Yet others say that Timeslips are linked to Psychometry. Psychometry says that every object contains its entire History. Getting in touch with the object, you are able to perceive its entire timeline. Timeslips then, are Psychometry with an entire place. One could therefore "trigger time travel" by being very interested in a place while the mind is relaxed.

While I do believe in psychometry and the merits of a relaxed mind, I believe that sensing a things History is not the same thing as making a leap into another time. At the very least, Timeslips would be an extreme form of Psychometry.

Psychometry itself can easily be taught, right here and now:

Touch an Object with the Intention to find something out about its History. Close your eyes.

That's it. I just taught you Psychometry. In a way, it is time travel into the past. Those sensitive to it, do receive flashes and images of the circumstances surrounding the object. Objects do contain all of that information. That's why we like to get rid of some and keep others.

It's also known that you can see the "astral realm" when you look with the outer left and right edges of your eyes. That allows you to see the auras of people. Sometimes you can see non-physical presences. And sometimes you will be able to see things that are located in other "times".

Another way to improve psychometric perception is by looking at something then looking away repeatedly or by focusing and de-focusing.

In any case, Timeslips differ from psychometry because you are not only perceiving something in mind, you are present physically and interacting with another time.

Are timeslips fun? Yes, usually they are. They can also be unsettling. My hunch is, having read this chapter means you too are destined to experience one or several timeslips in your life.

5

Secret Time Travel Technology

There are many conspiracy theories on Secret Time Travel Technology. I have read most of them. I'm not satisfied with any of them.

If there are people dedicated to utmost secrecy, then good information will be scarce and researchers fill in the blanks with imagination. People who sell fantasy as facts, I dislike the most, even more than those who keep stuff hidden.

The U.S. Military for example, is known to now be about 100 years ahead of the general populace in terms of technology and knowledge. They used the Internet several decades before we did, had supersonic planes long before the public knew and goodness knows what they have now. It's not satisfying to me personally, to be kept out of the loop of most what is actually going on in terms of advancement of humanity. That's why I know a little more than the average Joe. I know things by choice, because I looked, researched, asked and kept doing so. I don't expect to be handed knowledge without any effort on my part.

I also understand that disclosing too much to the public, weakens the position of those in power (or so they think). But the levels and layers of secrecy deployed by various organizations, such as the Military, has reached such peaks that fact and fantasy have become very difficult to discern.

An example: Do we have a secret space program that runs parallel to the public and official space program? Is the NASA just a front that is covering our "real" space program? To people unfamiliar with paranoid thinking, the question might sound bizarre. But there is some evidence that points to the possibility. Every couple of years a new fact floats up to public awareness and people wonder. For example, a decade ago, a Hacker by the name of Gary McKinnon hacked into Pentagon computers. Among many mundane things that he found, he also came across a list of "off world Navy Personnel". What's that? Who knew that the Navy employed personnel "off world"? The media didn't ask these questions and like so many other strange things, this brief peek into a secret project, faded out of awareness again.

To an outsider it is difficult to find out to what *extent* that space program has been deployed. Just for travel to the Moon or, as some claim, to other Solar Systems or even Galaxies?

To the extent of secret satellites or the extent of entire stealth spaceships? A few years ago, I looked into the topic and researched it. After a few months of writing on it, I dropped the whole subject and deleted the file I was writing. No book would be published. Why? Too convoluted. Too unclear. Too many contradictory reports and stories. And that's how you can tell someone really, desperately wants something kept under the lid – they put out a dozen contradictory stories on it.

According to a Wikipedia entry on Special Access Programs...

Special Access Programs (SAPs) in the U.S. Federal Government are security protocols that provide highly classified information with safeguards and access restrictions that exceed those for regular (collateral) classified information.

...

Two types of SAP exist—acknowledged and unacknowledged. The existence of an acknowledged SAP may be publicly disclosed, but the details of the program remain classified. An unacknowledged SAP (or USAP) is made known only to authorized persons, including members of the appropriate committees of the United States Congress. Waived SAPs are a subset of unacknowledged SAPs in the Department of Defense. These SAPs are exempt by statutory authority of the Secretary of Defense from most reporting requirements and, within the legislative branch, the only persons who are required to be informed of said SAPs are the chairpersons and ranking committee members of the Senate Appropriations Committee, Senate Armed Services Committee, House Appropriations Committee, and the House Armed Services Committee. Oftentimes, this notification is only oral.

https://en.wikipedia.org/wiki/Special_access_program

In other words, the Government entertains programs that are so secret they aren't even written down or acknowledged to exist. So, secret in fact, that most members of Government don't even know they exist. So secret, that it could give rise to rogue splinter groups that go do their own thing, outside of public accountability. It's one thing for the public not to know what is going on in their own country, but it's a whole other level of strange when not even elected officials can know what is going on. Such a country cannot be considered a Republic nor a Democracy.

Let's look at the Wikipedia entry on Black Projects and Black Budget:

A black project is a term used for a highly classified military or defense project publicly unacknowledged by government, military personnel, and contractors.

https://en.wikipedia.org/wiki/Black_project

A black budget is a government budget that is allocated for classified or other secret operations of a nation. The black budget is an account expenses and spending related to military research and covert operations. The black budget is mostly classified due to security reasons. The black budget can be complicated to *calculate, but in the United States it has been estimated to be over US$50 billion a year.*

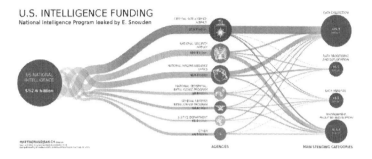

U.S. INTELLIGENCE FUNDING
National Intelligence Program leaked by E. Snowden

The United States Department of Defense has a black budget it uses to fund black projects—expenditures that it does not want to disclose publicly. The annual cost of the United States Department of Defense black budget was estimated at $30 billion in 2008, but was increased to an estimated $50 billion in 2009. A black budget article by The Washington Post, based on information given by Edward Snowden, detailed how the US allocated $52.8 billion in 2012 for the black budget.

The black budget has been known to hide multiple types of projects from elected officials. With secret code names and hidden figures, the details of the black budget are revealed only to certain people of congress, if at all.

This budget was approved by the US National Security Act of 1947, which created the Central Intelligence Agency, the National Security Council and reorganized some military bases with help of the Defense Department.

The U.S. Government claims that the money given to this budget investigates advanced sciences and technologies for military issues. This kind of research is responsible for the creation of new aircraft, weapons, and satellites.

https://en.wikipedia.org/wiki/Black_budget

The article goes on to say that the 2018 black budget was $81 Billion.

Here's something strange: On the "Black Projects" page, there is a short list of previously classified projects that have now been declassified. That list is so short it barely covers the budget of one or two years.

What that means is that there is an *enormous* amount of stuff Government money is being spent on of which we know nothing of. If we take 50 Billion as an average figure (and that's only the figure being disclosed or "publicly acknowledged") that adds up to *Trillions* of Dollars in the last few decades. Where does that money go? And that's only counting Black Projects in the United States. I'm sure Europe, Russia and China have similar happening.

In school, children learn that "The Government serves the public", that the Government is in fact the public. If that is true, then why is the public kept in the dark about the majority of the Governments expenses?

The excuse always sounds something like this: "We don't want the Russians or Chinese to get their hands on this! How irresponsible would that be!" But with *Trillions* being spent outside of public awareness or transparency, the secrecy has certainly gotten out of control a long time ago. That much money could easily build a fleet of off-world spaceships. It could build vast underground facilities. And maybe time machines? What follows are tales and claims around secret time travel technology. For each story I will explain why I believe, or in most cases, disbelieve a story.

Time Traveling Flying Saucers

I've seen flying saucers with my own eyes on a few occasions. I've also seen other unidentified aircraft performing maneuvers that known aircraft cannot perform. I have seen silver discs in the sky, I've seen them go into water and come out of it. Because so many others have meanwhile seen it, the topic of UFOs can now be considered mainstream. This is what people believe they are:

1. Alien Aircraft (30%)
2. Hallucinations or Psychological Phenomena (30%)
3. Aircraft of the Military, Government, Intelligence Agencies (20%)
4. Time Travelers or Dimensional Travelers (10%)
5. Secret Nazi Aircraft (2%)
6. Flying Discs from Inside Earth (1%)
7. Something Other (7%)

And here's what I believe they are: *Mostly Secret Human-Made Aircraft.* Well, to be honest, I don't "believe" that anymore, I know it. When I first wrote this book, I considered it. Meanwhile I know it for a fact. That's of course not to say that Aliens don't exist. The Universe is full of intelligent life. And yes, there is also the possibility that human-made flying saucers were inspired by alien craft. So, there's that.

The reason I bring the subject of flying saucers and UFOs up is because some researchers believe they are time machines by either humans or aliens from the future.

As a Teenager, I read about every book on UFOs on the Market. And I mean *every* book. When I want to know something, I can get quite obsessed about and read everything I can until the topic is completely exhausted. After reading most books on UFOs out there, I concluded that most of them were not written to inform, they were written to manipulate. By that, I mean they were written to cover up the Governments ownership of flying saucers, so that the saucers could be used to their advantage. Recently declassified documents have actually confirmed as much. The CIA and DIA published dozens of books on UFOs and Aliens in the 1950s, ostensibly to "research the belief systems of society". This little fact was not widely published when it was declassified, because frankly, it's *outrageous*. You have Millions of people thinking they are reading honest accounts of people who have encountered Aliens or whatever, when the books they read were actually made by shady propaganda office of an intelligence agency. Unfortunately, these three-letter-agencies that are meant to contribute to our

Intelligence are more often than not, contributing to our lack of intelligence

Regardless of whether UFOs are human made, alien or from other Dimensions, observers have noticed that some of these flying discs, flying tubes, flying triangles and flying balls have the ability to de- and rematerialize. As already implied, if someone can dematerialize and instantly appear in another space, they likely also have the ability to appear in another time. Mastery of space and time go together. Spacetime shouldn't actually be separate words, it should read "spacetime" in my view. What if some of these objects that display all these advanced flight skills, are our descendants (humans in the future)? That might explain why so many UFOs have been sighted over historically significant places.

My research leads me to believe that the human-made version of flying saucers was invented (or rediscovered) by the Austrian naturalist, Forrester and inventor Viktor Schauberger through his observation of Nature and development of vortex and implosion Technology. Schauberger had numerous drawings and models of flying saucers. Because of his work on them, he was invited to meet with Adolf Hitler personally. It is rumored that the Nazis stole his work and attempted to build flying saucers for themselves. After the war, he was invited by "U.S. Industrialists" with ties to the Military. Shortly after his meeting with the Americans, Schauberger died and his materials were stolen by them. His family testified to this.

Viktor Schauberger lived a hundred years ago and developed everything from vortex-based water energizers to flying saucers. Upon hearing that, the narrow-minded might call him a quack. But a quack is someone who invents nothing of good use. Schaubergers ideas have been implemented by people and companies for energy and money saving use. Water-twisters based on his ideas have found Millions of enthusiastic customers around the world.

"The majority believe that everything hard to comprehend must be very profound. This is incorrect. What is hard to understand is immature, unclear and often false. The highest wisdom is simple and passes through the brain, directly to the heart"

- Viktor Schauberger

I learned of his ideas about 30 years ago, in a book called "Living Water", but dismissed them because I couldn't fit them into any known category of my own work. The more I learned in my own field of study (consciousness and energy), the more his teachings appealed to me.

I know from my own out-of-body experiences that time, space and energy flow in spiral shapes, not in straight lines. Water flows in the same way, in a zig-zag rather than a straight line. The wind creates similar patterns on desert sand. Musical notes create the same shape. Our Galaxy is shaped as a spiral. The energy frequencies that everything flows from, follow the same patterns.

A documentary titled "Comprehend and Copy Nature" (which can be found for free online) is a good introduction and summary of his discoveries around energized water (vs. dead water), as well as the possibility of near-free-energy through anti-gravity devices. If you think that's "impossible", consider that all of nature runs on "free energy", the entire Universe is a perpetual motion device. But whether Schauberger really discovered free energy devices or not, he had extraordinary vision and this world could certainly use more of his type. He talked about clean technology long before the idea was mainstream and built flying saucer models long before anyone had seen them.

The reason the idea of vortex technology somehow relating to time travel appeals to me, is because I have personally experienced the tornado-like spin in my own time slips. I don't understand the science of it, but I've been through it a few times. Maybe there's more to the Wizard of Oz, in which Dorothy is transported to another Dimension on a Tornado. And maybe there's more to Alice in Wonderland, where Alice follows a "rabbit hole" into another world. All of this is also eerily reminiscent of what physicists say about wormholes and vortexes in regards to time travel. I clearly remember three instances in which my time jump was accompanied by a clockwise or counter-clockwise spinning sensation.

Interestingly, the Sufi Mystics of the Middle East and Persia believe that spinning is used to reach higher states of Consciousness or even Out-of-Body Experiences. Sufi Dervishes have been whirling for at least a thousand years.

I have observed flying discs spinning in the sky, with my own eyes.

Spinning is also how Seattle Attorney Andrew Basiago claims the U.S. Government travels through time…

Project Pegasus

Andrew Basiago, who actually ran for President in 2016, promising to disclose secret time travel Technology, claims that he participated in "Project Pegasus" between the ages 7 and 12. This is fairly consistent with other time travel claims in which it is said that children are the better time travelers. Why children? Probably because their consciousness isn't fixated. Which would confirm that time travel cannot be done without the right consciousness. Some of these stories however, take a darker turn, when they speak of children being *abducted* for experiments. I certainly hope that's not true.

Project Pegasus, he says, is a secret program for time travel and teleportation, run by the Defense Advanced Research Project Agency (DARPA).

Basiago describes different types of time travel technologies. One of them is a teleportation device by Nikola Tesla.

"The machine consisted of two gray elliptical booms about eight feet tall, separated by about 10 feet, between which a shimmering curtain of what Tesla called 'radiant energy' was broadcast," Basiago said. "Radiant energy is a form of energy

that Tesla discovered that is latent and pervasive in the universe and has among its properties the capacity to bend time-space."

This radiant energy shimmered white and blue, sometimes a peculiar turquoise. Participants walked through the energy field into a vortex tunnel. When the vortex closed, they found themselves at the destination. The "white and blue shimmer", by the way, is consistent with various tales of time portals, ancient and new. As there is no way for me to confirm or deny stories such as these, I look for whether they are or are not consistent whether other things I know.

"One felt either as if one was moving at a great rate of speed or moving not at all, as the universe was wrapped around one's location," Basiago says.

Another time travel method has a person lying down on a spinning table with legs and arms spread out. The person lying on the spinning table is looking to the ceiling to which a spiral shape is attached. The body is spun in one direction and the spiral in the other direction, creating a vortex in consciousness. Says Basiago:

"If you put somebody on a tabletop, in a 'Da Vinci Vitruvian Man' kind of body position but with their head in the center of the circle, and have them look up at an image of a spiral on the ceiling while they are being spun clockwise at 33 rotations per minute, you can train them to go out of body".

Image: Basiago explains Spinning

This is actually true and lends some credence to Basagios claims. I have consciously left the body hundreds of times it usually goes along with spinning sensations. Does that mean all of Basiagos claims are true? No. But at the very least, he knows some stuff.

Basiago makes many other claims, significantly more outrageous, such as going to Mars with Obama or having photographic evidence of travelling back to Lincolns Gettysburg address in 1863 multiple times. Unfortunately, these claims are unverifiable, unlike the spinning techniques, which are experientially verifiable. I'll quote from an Internet article on him nonetheless:

Basiago claimed he can be seen in a photograph of Abraham Lincoln at Gettysburg in 1863, which he said he visited in 1972 via a plasma confinement chamber located in East Hanover, N.J.

*"I had been dressed in period clothing, as a Union bugle boy,"
he said. "I attracted so much attention at the Lincoln speech site
at Gettysburg — wearing over-sized men's street shoes — that I
left the area around the dais and walked about 100 paces over
to where I was photographed in the Josephine Cogg image of
Lincoln at Gettysburg." (The boy on the left in the photo below).*

*In addition, Basiago said he traveled to Ford's Theatre the night
of Lincoln's assassination on five or six occasions. "I did not,
however, witness the assassination," he said. "Once, I was on the
theater level when he was shot and I heard the shot followed by
a great commotion that arose from the crowd. It was terrible to
hear."*

*Basiago said each of his visits to the past was different, "like they
were sending us to slightly different alternative realities on
adjacent timelines. As these visits began to accumulate, I twice
ran into myself during two different visits."*

*Being sent back in time to the same place and moment, but from
different starting points in the present, allowed two of himselves
to be in Ford's Theatre at the same time in 1865.*

*"After the first of these two encounters with myself occurred, I
was concerned that my cover might be blown," he recalled.
"Unlike the jump to Gettysburg, in which I was clutching a
letter to Navy Secretary Gideon Welles to offer me aid and
assistance in the event I was arrested, I didn't have any
explanatory materials when I was sent to Ford's Theatre."*

*And how did these alleged time travelers return to the present
day or their point of origin? According to Basiago, some sort of*

holographic technology allowed them to travel both physically and virtually.

"If we were in the hologram for 15 minutes or fewer," he explained, "the hologram would collapse, and after about 60 seconds of standing in a field of super-charged particles ... we would find ourselves back on the stage ... in the present."

Basiago said the technology should only be used for real-time teleportation, not time travel, because, "It would be chaos."

Is Project Pegasus real or not? I don't know. Like with so many of these tales, I am sure *things like this* are real, without knowing whether this particular story is real.

But I do know that time travel has to do with spinning. Most people who first attempt to spin like the Sufi Mystics feel nauseous. It can take some practice to achieve such inner balance that the motion is more of a flow. I personally do not practice spinning due to the simple fact that I don't enjoy it. With me, the spinning-sensation does not occur physically, it happens energetically.

Why is time travel linked to spinning? I suspect its to do with the spiral nature of time. Just because time is not linear, does not mean it doesn't have any shape at all. If time had a shape, it would be spiral. The spinning then, indicates quickly going up or down a spiral into another time. Do all time slips or out of body experiences involve spinning? No. But when I have experienced it, it was always connected to leaving my body or time.

The Montauk Project

The Montauk Project was published in the 1990s. The whole story is rather bizarre. I don't personally believe it because it's not consistent with other things I know and also because the authors of the Montauk books don't strike me as trustworthy or especially interested in diligent research. Their books are sensationalistic and exaggerated, written more like fiction than fact. I briefly present it here anyway, because it's a part of popular time-travel lore. I originally read all of the Montauk series because I enjoy books that obscure the line between fiction and reality. In the 1990s, four books on Montauk were published. I'm not sure if more have been published because I stopped following the story. The constantly increasing number of books, magazines, newsletters, websites, audio programs and merchandise of the authors, made it clear that they are more marketers than genuine journalists and researchers.

The Montauk Project speaks of secret time travel experiments of the U.S Government in Montauk, a former military base at the edge of Long Island, New York. They connect it to everything from the Invisibility Cloak of the Philadelphia Experiment to Teleportation, Brainwashing and Mind Control, Abduction of Teenagers and Children that were forced to be lab rats through Drugs and Torture, futuristic gadgets used for remote influence of people, Nikola Tesla, Albert Einstein, van Neumann, UFOs, ESP, Time-Space Laboratories, Weather Control, Wilhelm Reich, The

Pleiades, Aleister Crowley, L. Ron Hubbard, several U.S. Presidents, Nazis working for the U.S., crashed UFOs in Germany, subterranean civilizations, Stealth Technology, the Akashic Chronicles, the Face on Mars, numerous U.S. Universities that were involved, etc.

The books are essentially a "name dropping" orgy, meant to appeal to lovers of conspiracy theories. Not a single theory is left out. I do believe that any and all of that is quite possible and quite possibly real. I just don't believe that the authors really know about it or even experienced any of it. As popular as these books are in time travel circles, I wouldn't recommend them. They contain nothing useful to a person who wishes to experience themselves beyond time.

Wingmakers

The Wingmakers Project started in 1998 and its website wingmakers.com is still up and running in 2020. I personally suspect this is just as fake as the Montauk Project, but on a higher level. I'd classify it as an art project rather than a time travel project. Nonetheless, it is part of time travel lore on the Internet.

Wingmakers is a collection of aesthetic paintings, musical works and semi-sophisticated philosophies.

According to the website, an NSA scientist by the pseudonym of Dr. Anderson was said to be working for a "Project Broken Arrow". The Project was to salvage and decipher a "time capsule" that was buried by an advanced civilization in the caves of Arizona, waiting for its rediscovery for thousands of years. A time capsules purpose is to survive for a long time to send a message to future generations (some speculate that the Giza Pyramids themselves are time capsules). These time capsules contained golden discs that were deciphered by NSA cartographers. They contained a writing unknown on earth and their deciphering unveiled philosophy and poetry of another civilization, several unusual paintings and fascinating music. According to Dr. Anderson, some people within the NSA had the theory that the capsule was not placed by people from the past but that the Wingmakers were time travelling people from the future who were sent to the past. In spite of secrecy agreements, Dr. Anderson pushed for the information to be made public. He offered the materials to a journalist, who initially didn't know what to do with it. Dr. Anderson insisted that he wished to stay anonymous and did not desire to personally profit from the story. While the journalist was still thinking about what to do with the story, the scientist disappeared and left her all the material. For her safety, she copied the material and put it in a safe, ordering that it should be send around the whole world if she also disappeared. Then she created a website with the Material, featuring the story of the Broken Arrow Project, the Philosophy of the Wingmakers, the Paintings and the Music and other background information.

I wrote the above paragraph in 2001. I was already skeptical back then, as much as I enjoyed the Wingmakers material, but meanwhile Wingmakers themselves have confirmed it to be a kind of *philosophy-and-art-project* and the Time Capsules, Time Travel and NSA Story to be nothing more than "fictionalized myth making". I include the case in this book to remind any reader to keep a dose of healthy skepticism when looking into this kind of stuff.

Project Looking Glass

The following so "far out there", that even if just 10% of it is true, everything we ever knew about anything at all needs to be questioned and re-written. And that's the problem with many of these stories. Either humanity has been led totally astray about the nature of reality, or it's someone making stuff up. There is hardly a middle ground on tales such as this.

The following is partially quoted from here: http://www.projectcamelot.org/dan_burisch_summary.html

Dr. Burisch was a Senior Operative/Scientist, responsible first to the Committee of the Majority and the Majestic 12 (1986-2003), then only to the Majestic 12 (2003-2005), before it was adjourned (October 12, 2005).

During the 1991 Gulf War, he was assigned to a Black/Ops Unit, and was deployed into the International Coalition's Zone of Operations, for the purpose of counteracting a rogue military unit's intended application of unauthorized biological warfare agents against the Iraqi Army.

After his return, he was ultimately assigned as a 'Microbiologist V' at the Papoose Lake Facility (S4) and operated as a Working Group Leader on Project Aquarius, where his responsibilities included leading a group of scientists in the investigation of a 'J-Rod's' (extraterrestrial entity's) neuropathy. Such investigation included his being introduced into a Clean Sphere containment unit and interacting directly with the J-Rod, then processing, evaluating, and transforming tissue samples for reintroduction into the J-Rod, with the intent to ameliorate the pathology.

In the late 1990s, Dr. Burisch was formally censured by the Committee of the Majority for his violation of direct orders, but had his academic credentials restored in 2006 by intervention of a very private Religious order, based in France. (His credentials may be verified upon request.) During 2005, for a short time, Dr. Burisch sat as a pro-tem member of the Majestic 12, as MJ-9, and was finally assigned as H-1-Maj, the designated person to disclose the "extraterrestrial human lineage (time travel) information". He completed his final orders in September, 2006, and is retired from service.

In June 2007 he was asked my the new Majestic group to participate for several months in a special project concerning issues of "National Security", which invitation he accepted. This assignment lasted until 14 December, 2007.

Dan's experiences with Extraterrestrials, and Majestic-12, go back about 20 years. He was inducted into Majestic in 1986, while he was a student at UNLV. Even before he was at UNLV he had a long and distinguished history in microbiology, working for many years with the Los Angeles Microscopical Society, and studying with Dr. John Bunyan (England)1, so Majestic knew he was gifted.

They offered him an opportunity to work in BlackOps, in his specialty, and become well respected in Special Applications and the chance to further his education into areas he'd only dreamed about. So he said 'yes' and found himself being trained and groomed to work up at Area-51 on 'exotic' biological materials.

At that time, Dan did not know that he was in fact being 'mentored' by one of the highest ranking members of the Majestic-12, who felt (and still continues to feel) a great affection and connection to Dan because of the events surrounding Dan's abduction in the early 1970s. While working on exotics Dan (by then, Dr. Dan Crain, having completed his Ph.D) learned that the tissue he had been studying was in-fact Extraterrestrial in nature.

Dan found that he was being given a surprising measure of leeway, while working within the facility. He was still required to follow all the protocols, however his badge (as we later learned) was keyed to allow him access to multiple levels within the laboratory complexes at both Area-51 and S-4.4 This permitted him a range of movement, and access to other projects rarely enjoyed by those working in highly structured Special Application environments.

Dan became familiar with a project called 'Looking Glass' which involved a back-engineered Extraterrestrial device originally designed to be a portal opening mechanism for

Stargate-type travel - which had (has) the capacity to bend time/space so that events over the forward and rear event horizons could be viewed. When it is paired up with a second device using the settings, events can not only be viewed but heard and more. This device was also being tested for communications protocols and transportation applications as recently as 2003-2004 before being dismantled for safety reasons as we enter further into the highly energetic space in and around the galactic plane.

While being introduced to these other projects, Dan began to work as part of the Aquarius-J-Rod team6 which was tasked with the problem of figuring out why the J-Rods (commonly called Grays) were suffering from a debilitating medical condition that affected their nerves. Part of this work involved taking physical tissue samples from the J-Rod housed deep below S-4 in a 'Clean Sphere' designed to support his atmospheric and environmental needs.

It soon became apparent that these Extraterrestrials were not all that different from us. In fact, as communications improved, it was learned that they are not so much space travelers as time/space travelers, using a small planet in the Gliese System as a local base (approximately 15 light years from Earth) where they can stage for their trips here. Using Looking Glass technology (which might be more properly called Stargate technology) they traveled in time from a Human future, which is real to them, but only potential for us...

...

"With regard to LG (Looking Glass): As I understand it, this device (at least 3 to 4 years ago) could not focus on a detailed sequence of activities in the future. In other words, you could not see exactly what would happen, like a series of events.

I was told to consider the multiverse idea combined with work by Richard Gott on cosmic strings.

The multiverse apparently is accessed when the forward mode is set. I was also told to consider the views provided by Looking Glass as one of many potential realities (at least in the future view mode).

I have also been told that recently there has been an effort made to outfit videotape recorders to be sent forward through the apparatus, thereby allowing the dark project people to gain some insight into what may take place.

When I heard about this several questions came to my mind. The most pressing of which was: if a camera were sent forward in time/space, would it be able to record anything other than what was immediately in front of its lens? I mean, what if Looking Glass were located in the middle of the Groom Lake facility, and the operators wanted to gain insight into the outcome of a conflict, say in the Middle East.

How could a videotape recorder, set to record what was right in front of its lens at that location gather any data on the Middle East if it were still stuck in the middle of the Mojave desert when it got to the future??? Hell, something important could be happening right behind the camera and it would miss it - a couple of degrees change in camera direction allows one set of events to be seen while another set is completely overlooked, much less events half a world away.

To answer this question, my contact was not specific, saying only that cameras did not move, as mass does not change in its perspective to space time. However, such an item placed into the injected atmosphere, might experience a different time, if only briefly. And cameras could film within the gas or see images in the injected atmosphere as though it were a lens reflecting events in and around the column. I was given to understand that the tilt or positioning of the electromagnets would allow different views or positions in the environment to be reflected in the gas column.

(I feel confident that at least two rings of electromagnets are employed and that the rest of the device is composed of a barrel and the gas injected into the barrel - Two different sources have indicated that these are the basic components - These magnets spin in different directions, creating a charge of some kind.

Then the gas is injected into the barrel. Depending on the direction of the spin - I am sure speed and tilt and a bunch of other factors must also have an effect - time space can be warped forward or backwards by long or short distances relative to the present. I have reason to believe that the scientists have completed a map of the exact positions and speeds of the magnets necessary to reach targeted times both forward and back.)

Apparently, images of the events at different places, relative to the location of the device can be picked up and in essence *reflected off the gas, causing it to behave like a teleprompter or crystal ball, for lack of a better example*

But I am not entirely sure that mass does not move, or that mass is not affected.

Since I was also told many years ago about an experiment that went very wrong in the early years of the Looking Glass project, involving a test subject of some kind. As I understand it there was significant movement of mass during that experiment, and it ended up with a rather gruesome death for the poor test subject.

(I originally thought it was a monkey, but I found out that there were many test subjects that got sent through, so I am not certain what kind was involved in the experiment that went bad. However, in my typical reverse-logic search for corollaries, this tells me that there must have been many test subjects that made it through just fine. So, I am certain that any errors that were made or any miscalculations have long since been corrected).

I wish I could offer you more information.

For what its worth, my sources have confirmed the presence of electromagnets and a barrel-like device which is injected with some kind of gas....these components seem necessary for Looking Glass to function as a viewing device. And as for any changes in mass, or movement within time-space.... I really don't know since my information sources would only tell me 'so much' about what they saw or experienced at the time they were involved.

But it can be reasoned, based upon what they did say that there were significant experiments in the movement of mass back and forward through time, many of which were successful. I am sure much has been discovered and/or refined in the process since then."

There is more online, I just present a few snippets. It's all very interesting, entertaining even. But is it true? I doubt it. In one of his Video Interviews, Dan Burish does say that the information of what is seen in the "Looking Glass" changes according to a person's consciousness. That's just about the only piece of information I'm able to confirm.

Readers might be disappointed that I'm being as skeptical as I am. Please understand that my skepticism doesn't come from a non-believers place. I wholeheartedly believe in Time Travel and even the possibility that there are gadgets for it. I also believe that there are Shadow Governments outside of public awareness or control. Most media-hyped "Skepticism", comes from people who would never believe, people with an agenda to debunk. That's not my skepticism.

It's possible that there is a *Project Looking Glass*. Consider all the fairy tales in which witches and psychics saw the future in their round glasses or witch balls. Those fairy tales must be founded in some kind of reality.

The problem is that there are many people reporting of various secret Government Projects of different names, involving different people and different locations. Most of these stories are logically consistent within themselves, *but when comparing them to other stories, there are several things that don't add up. In other words, at least some of these secret project reports must be false.* It is difficult to contrast and compare this information with other accounts and reports of secret projects, because we do not know which previous project is true vs. false.

I do not want to imply that any of these things are true, because they could easily be total fabrications. Nor do I want to categorically say any tale of mystery and cover-up must be false, because I myself have experienced a lot of unexplained things in my life.

Until we have specific evidence, all of the stories are not useful other than for entertainment and perhaps inspiration.

Another possibility I find likely, is that at least some of these stories are put out their by agencies to *cover up* what is really going on. There might be something amazing happening, but all these nonsensical stories serve to dissuade people from looking any further. For example, Looking Glass might refer to a top secret laser or energy beam that has the power to disintegrate nuclear weapons. So that the perceived enemy doesn't find out, people put out rumors about time travel.

In fact, I have an acquaintance who has worked for several intelligence agencies tell me, that it is standard operating procedure to put out several false stories around any secret project!

So if you find several contradicting stories around a reported secret Government project, you know there really is something going on, but it's not whatever the story says it is.

Remote Viewing

For most of us, learning Remote Viewing is more useful than relying on becoming a member of some secret club that runs a time machine. Remote Viewing is the ability to see, perceive or sense that which is not in your immediate surroundings.

"Mainstream" Institutions such as Universities or Wikipedia still claim there is "no evidence" for this ability and label anyone claiming so a "Charlatan". On the other hand, the Russian, Chinese and U.S. Governments have invested heavily in researching and developing ESP (Extrasensory Perception). In the U.S. the CIA, NSA DIA, DEA and the FBI have actively recruited and worked with psychics and developed official Remote Viewing Protocols. They have solicited Princeton and Stanford University scientists and other scholars for their research. Remote Viewing has been used in Military Intelligence for decades. You can read more about this in books by Joseph McMoneagle, especially books around Project Stargate (the books "Mind Trek" "Remote Viewing Secrets" for instance).

Toward the public, remote viewing is trashed as "pseudo-science", but in reality, it is an important part of the Governments work. The secrecy obviously by design. Just like "Governments" like to hoard the latest technology for themselves and to their advantage, they like to keep abilities such as remote viewing to themselves. But learning it is your personal choice. And if you wish to time travel, you can, regardless of what anyone is or isn't covering up.

The most interesting of Joseph McMoneagles books for our purposes is "The Ultimate Time Machine". It explains how Remote Viewing is applied to time travel, just like in this book. If you wish to learn more about the background of time travel in consciousness, that's the book to refer to. In this book I have not focused on the military history of time-remote-viewing but rather on methods to learn the skill itself. In any case, it's one of the few secret time travel experiments of the Government that can be proven and verified.

6

The Physics of Time Travel

"Imagination is more important than knowledge" – Albert Einstein

The official and popular stance of Science does not interest me all that much, because I don't believe that our contemporary knowledge is very advanced. I have gained far more advanced experience through the study of Spirituality. The Infinite Self is beyond time and space. A human being first learns to travel through space. And then through time. And then a human re-discovers the Self beyond time and space. "Science" is many decades far away from even such basic knowledge. That said, I'll provide a rough overview of scientific thought on the subject, just for the sake of comparison.

Modern physics acknowledges that time travel is theoretically possible. In 1905, Albert Einstein introduced relativity theory and proposed a speed that could bend time. Time, he said, is not an unchangeable constant, it can be stretched or condensed. In 1916, Einstein demonstrated that not only Speed but also Gravity could bend Space-Time. Einstein's publications were a breakthrough in the public's view of the Universe. Despite these widely acknowledged facts, most people still live their lives as if time were a fixed constant.

In 1937 Kurt Godel suggested that the entire Universe is a Time Machine. His Model of the Universe included possibilities for time travel. In 1949 he showed that one could travel time through "closed time curves". Extreme Gravity could bend Time-Space in a way that time would loop back on itself, into the past. Godels work was the first that explained time travel without contradicting any known physical or mathematical laws.

Modern physicists say that wormholes can transport us into past or future. Some say that time travel creates the paradoxical problem of mixing up cause and effect. One could get rich quick by acquiring the lottery numbers or stock market numbers one week ahead of time. One could use faster-than-light particles (Tachyons) like radio waves to get the information.

Physicists like to say that anything that is not expressly forbidden by natural laws, can happen. I'd like to add that anything that is possible will actually be done. If cloning humans is possible, there will be someone, somewhere, doing it. As the laws of physics support time travel in principle, physicists have been looking for ways to make it possible. The most popular idea of the last 70 years has been that of Wormholes. Wormholes can theoretically shorten extreme distances and also enable time travel. General relativity theory can make exact predictions about the flow of time on both ends of a wormhole. There are two ends to a wormhole, the entrance is in motion, the other is still. Because of time dilation, watches go slower at an entrance/opening that is in motion than at a still opening. That's true when viewing the wormhole from outside of it, but from within the wormhole, time passes the same.

What this means in layman terms is that, if the funds and technology were available, one could turn a wormhole into a time machine.

An Example: A space traveler finds a small wormhole in space and flies into one end of it at near light-speed. If he turns around and goes back to the entrance, his twin brother might have aged 20 years while he hasn't aged at all. He's travelled 20 years into the future. This is Einstein's twin paradox, according to which time moves slower for an astronaut in a fast spaceship than for his twin brother on earth. The time discrepancy can be reversed through the wormhole as well. The brother left behind moves through the moving opening of the wormhole and as soon as his brother returns, he gets back to his own younger self that was just left by his twin brother. The only limitation with Wormholes is, that it wouldn't be possible to travel to a past that is further back than the time it was first used as a time machine. Vice versa, the twin brother who got younger, can enter the still part of the Wormhole and travel to the future.

Physicists no longer consider three-dimensional space and time as separate things, but rather as different aspects of a four-dimensional space-time. Quantum Physicists who study subatomic particles have noted that time can probably move forward and backward.

The gravity of a Black Hole is so large, that it can turn any space-time-construct into a singularity. The singularity is a ring shape in time-space, the whole in the middle allows for the travel to another place or time.

For a civilization that could harness the energy of black holes, time travel would be easy. The astronomer Frank Tipler made a formula for it: Take 1 piece of matter with 10 sun-masses, push them together and roll them into a long, thin, super compact cylinder, like a black hole in the shape of spaghetti. Then rotate the structure a few Billion rotations a Minute and see what happens. Tipler says that a spaceship that is on a precisely calculated spiral trajectory around the cylinder, would enter a closed, time-like curve that would transport it Billions of years and numerous galaxies far away from the original location.

Some physicists have said that light itself could be used to travel time. If one could reduce a circulating light beam to be extremely slow, it could open a portal to the past. Physicist Ronald Mallett from the University of Connecticut, claims to be building a time machine based on this principle. In order to make light this slow, one requires temperatures at absolute zero (273,15 Celsius Minus). Later, Mallett discarded the idea of slowing down light in favor of other methods.

Quoted from Wikipedia:

https://en.wikipedia.org/wiki/Ronald_Mallett

In 1975, Mallett was appointed a job as assistant professor at the University of Connecticut. He was promoted to the rank of full professor in 1987 and has received multiple academic honors and distinctions. His research interests include black holes, general relativity, quantum cosmology, relativistic astrophysics and time travel. As of 2018, he is a Professor Emeritus of Physics at the University of Connecticut.

Time travel research

For quite some time, Ronald Mallett has been working on plans for a time machine. This technology would be based upon a ring laser's properties in the context of Einstein's general theory of relativity. Mallett first argued that the ring laser would produce a limited amount of frame-dragging which might be measured experimentally, saying:

"In Einstein's General Theory of Relativity, both matter and energy can create a gravitational field. This means that the energy of a light beam can produce a gravitational field. My current research considers both the weak and strong gravitational fields produced by a single continuously circulating unidirectional beam of light. In the weak gravitational field of an unidirectional ring laser, it is predicted that a spinning

neutral particle, when placed in the ring, is dragged around by the resulting gravitational field."

In a later paper, Mallett argued that at sufficient energies, the circulating laser might produce not just frame-dragging but also closed timelike curves (CTC), allowing time travel into the past:

For the strong gravitational field of a circulating cylinder of light, I have found new exact solutions of the Einstein field equations for the exterior and interior gravitational fields of the light cylinder. The exterior gravitational field is shown to contain closed timelike lines.

The presence of closed timelike lines indicates the possibility of time travel into the past. This creates the foundation for a time machine based on a circulating cylinder of light.

Funding for his program, now known as the Space-time Twisting by Light (STL) project, is progressing. Full details on the project, Mallett's theories, a list of upcoming public lectures and links to popular articles on his work can be found at the Mallett's faculty web page, and an illustration showing the concept on which Mallett has designed the time machine can be seen here.

Mallett also wrote a book entitled, Time Traveler: A Scientist's Personal Mission to Make Time Travel a Reality, co-written with author Bruce Henderson, that was first published in 2006.

In 2006, Mallett declared that time travel into the past would be possible in the 21st century and possibly within a decade.

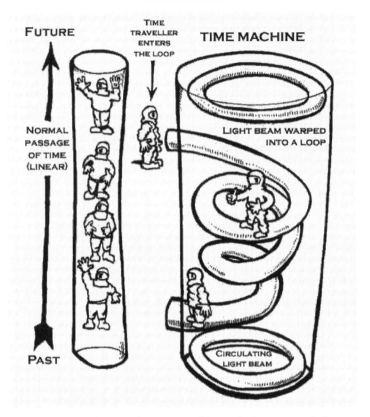

That was a peek into the status of knowledge around the start of the 21st Century. At least as far as the public is concerned. My own sense is, that none of this is anything new. If time travel exists, then it has always existed. It has existed a thousand years ago, 50 000 years ago, a Million years ago.

7

Non-Linear Causality

The following lecture is transcribed and updated from my 2018 Video "Non-Linear Causality". The original Lecture can be viewed online in the Video of the same name. It was a lecture on Success in Life, but it directly relates to time travel in that it teaches that time is not linear.

What was there first – the chicken or the egg? Neither. They arose simultaneously. I assert that Cause and Effect are identical and simultaneous. In fact, it's been one of the secrets in my success as a success-coach. I call this non-linear causality.

Non-linear causality is when you do a good thing and then another good thing happens. You go feed the birds and somebody gives you a job. There's no apparent direct relation between the two, but from a higher perspective, there is a correspondence.

Imagine seeing a race between a turtle and a car. The turtle gets a one hour or a 10- kilometer head start, but the whole race is 100 kilometers. You already know who will win. The car is will win because the turtle is too slow. But if you take snapshots of the race in the first hour it's will look as if the turtle is faster than the car, because you don't have the whole movie, you don't see the big picture you just see specific items at one point in time.

With a birds-eye-view, you see that an activity you do, may not have an instant gain it does have a long-term gain, and so you let go of the need for instant gratification. You choose to do the right thing instead of what's expedient. That's the way we're spiritually tested - is he going to do what's expedient and what gives them quick gain or is he going to do the right thing? Doing the right thing may be painful or hard or difficult just from looking at the snapshot but in seeing the entire movie you'll see that doing the right thing always leads to more good for yourself and others. It's only a matter of time before bad deeds come back to you. This is called cause and effect, Karma, law of attraction. Cause and effect may be years apart. You never know because consciousness does not operate in linear time. The mind does but consciousness does not, so ten years or one minute don't make much difference to consciousness.

Another way cause and effect are one and the same is that when a person reacts in a certain way to an event, it is not that the reaction was caused by the event but that the inner emotion *attracted the event* and the event re-triggered the emotion. In other words, the reaction was there prior to the event. As strange as that sounds to most people, its entirely true. If someone gets furiously angry at the slightest misstep or accident, the anger was already there prior to the misstep. The angry person claims that the misstep "caused" him or her to be angry, but by their over-reaction you can tell that something was already boiling within them before anything happened. They were merely looking for an external event to justify letting their anger burst out. It is likely that their already-existing anger played a part in attracting the misstep or accident. If I drop a normal glass of water and it shatters on the floor and another person throws a temper tantrum, you can be sure that the person has issues and had issues prior to the event of the glass falling. But people love blaming specific events for their own emotional shortcomings.

That's not to say that all emotional outbursts have no validity. But you will find that they are often not proportionate to the event and the person has a few other issues and they are using the event to let all these issues come to the surface. You make one sly remark and the other person goes into crisis-mode for several days even though you profusely apologize. That has nothing to do with the event and all to do with their already existing thoughts and emotions. What then, is an example of a legitimate emotional reaction? It is spontaneous and wasn't there prior to the event. Someone gets hurt and you genuinely worry. You witness someone being scammed and you get angry for a moment. You know its genuine if it is spontaneous rather than having been brooding for hours or even days.

People often ask me how much time it's going to take until their goal manifests, but the question itself is based on ideas that contradict how consciousness works. Either a goal is "already manifest" in consciousness right now, or it isn't. If something is already real within, you don't ask how long it will take to manifest. And that, in one little paragraph, is the secret of reality creation (for more on this, see my book *Reality Creation and Manifestation*).

When someone is sick, we sometimes ask what *caused* the sickness as if it were only one cause, one direct linear relation rather than a correspondence. When somebody has a car accident, we ask what *caused* it and we hardly ever ask about the causes, plural. We ask how things happened, as in "how did this idiot become a millionaire?". Such questions imply linear causality. Sure, every action has a consequence and for every action there's a reaction. I'm not saying there is no cause and effect. But in the bigger picture, it's more than just linear and most things have *multiple causes*. And here's another important side-note regarding reality creation: If there are numerous causes for something or numerous reasons why something should happen then it likely will happen.

A few examples of why it's not accurate to only think in linear terms of A to B to C causality:

I once had a Coaching Session with a doctor who felt guilty because she forgot to check a certain item for one of her seriously ill patients. Strictly speaking, it wasn't through her forgetfulness but through her ignorance that she didn't check because she didn't know she had to check. She was not guilty of wrongdoing in any way. But she felt guilty, thinking it was her fault if the patients' health were to decline and he eventually died.

I explained to her that it's not that simple. If the patient died, what caused it? Is it that the doctor forgot a little detail or is it the fact that this patient led an unhealthy lifestyle for many years? Or maybe he's been living with a nagging wife for years and that caused his illness. Or perhaps it was a certain food he ate that caused it. Maybe some bad chemicals in his surroundings. Or maybe it was just his time to die.

The patient hadn't even died yet, nor had the patient's situation gotten worse than it already was. In any case, it could not possibly be "the doctors fault", it would normally have multiple causes that all correspond to each other in a certain energy field. If this patient resides in a certain energy field or attitude, he's going to attract various events – one could be the nagging wife, another might be the illness and then on top of that he might also attract an incompetent doctor. Or what if it's the superior of that doctor who is to "blame"? What I am saying is that it's an entire field or context that attracts multiple so-called causes. Singular things aren't in and of themselves "cause". All cause is non-physical, arising from various fields of consciousness. I was actually surprised this highly educated doctor struggled to understand this. She was so mired in guilt that she projected it onto situations that didn't even warrant guilt.

That's not to say that we do not have personal responsibility. That's not what is being said at all. She is responsible for her part in the patients' overall story, responsible for her actions, responsible for her perceptions and reactions and for how she proceeds. And if she feels she made a mistake, it's the responsible thing to fess up to it and do a better job next time. That's responsibility. But that's different than guilt-tripping yourself over things you have no or very little effect on. She is responsible for doing the best she can with the patient, but the patient is responsible for years of self-neglect and changing his act when he gets released home.

Another example. You go to the mall. There, you slip on the wet floor and break your arm. What was the cause of that? Legally you might say it's the wet floor or you might say it's the guy who was supposed to put up a sign wet floor and that he failed to do his job. You see, lawyers are in the Business of manipulating perception of cause. If a lawyer can assign the lack of a sign as "cause", then the whole company running the mall can be sued for a lot of money.

But it could also be the taxi driver who went the wrong way causing you to come late to the mall causing you to slip on the floor because a it had just been done. You could say it's caused by your bad shoes which easily slip. Or it's caused by your own unawareness. You could say it's caused by the mall manager himself who laid the wrong floors. In such examples you see the nonsense of the "linear causality" ideology. Cause and Effect are not quite as set in stone as we think and we'd be well advised to acknowledge unseen influences. The linear mind thinks that A leads to B lead to C but in reality, the ABC (the entire field) is already present as an energy. Success and Failure are already present in the seed, in the initial idea, attitude or intention. ABC is one thing that manifests itself in various A-B-C events on a timeline. Events that appear separate from each other, belong together and arise together. A bad mood belongs to the late taxi, belongs to the irresponsible mall who failed to put up a sign, belongs to the worn-out shoes, etc.

This may all sound abstract and strange, but its quite practical. It means that once you have adjusted the essence of who you are, the general energy field, all kinds of corresponding ABCDEFG will show up and *spread out over a time line* for you. That's why it really is accurate to say "*Every battle is won before its begun*". Anybody who deeply understands just that statement, understands how reality works. Another way to say it is "*Well begun is half done*". I'd go further and say that well begun is completely done. Whether something is going to succeed or not is already determined and decided right now, in your energy field, your mental attitude. By the way you feel and act today, you can predict and determine what will be happening in the next weeks and months. You know this is true when you look at certain people who fail in whatever they touch and other people who succeed in whatever they do. Some people just fail and fail and fail and fail some succeed in anything. The funny thing is that the failure and the success might outwardly be doing the same thing. You can't just go and look at a successful person and copy what they're doing and imitate how they dress. That's beside the point even though a lot of motivational teachers teach that you can be successful by doing the same thing as successful people. But it's not about what they are doing or saying, it's about who they are as an overall energy field, belief-system and states of emotion. Some of this will express itself in actions, but actions are only the outermost, visible part of the whole. Success is determined by invisible things such as principles, values and inner states. These set the blueprint for later behaviors, reactions and even to what one perceives and fails to perceive. I see opportunity and benefit everywhere I go. That's not because of an inherent quality of physical reality but because of *who is looking*.

Don't go after the external manifestations of success, go for the underlying principles and attitudes of success. They have been known for thousands of years and haven't changed, because essence never changes. The rules of success that worked 5000 years ago 2,000 years ago hundred years ago will still work in 100 years and 10 000 years.

Once you understand how things work, that can't be taken away from you. That's just like having learned a language, it stays with you. Within a certain energy-field, things just happen spontaneously as part of that context. Imagine a river stream and there's fish swimming, fish jumping around. One fish is jumping on the left another fish is jumping on the right and that's *just what fish do in the river stream.* It's not that the river "causes" them to jump or that one fish "causes" the other to jump. That's what fish do. The causality has been set long before the stream or the fish came into existence. That's what being a fish in a river means - swimming around and jumping up and down.

You plant a seed in soil and a plant grows. Coming from linear causality you'd say "well what caused that? Was it the person planting the seed was it the seed, was it the seed in the soil, was it the soil was it the Sun, was it the rain?"

You see how ridiculous this "cause and effect" doctrine sounds? And yet, our entire "scientific paradigm" is built around this nonsense. If you hadn't planted the seed, would it have fallen there and grown by itself? Yes, it would. Trees grew long before people planted them. And yes, you can "cause" a tree to grow by planting it. But even if you don't, trees are still going to grow, because the context called "Planet Earth" allows for that in the right soil, the right weather and the right seeds.

All this may seem obvious to you. But most people really do live their lives as if it were a linear progression of hours, days, weeks, months and years. They firmly believe, that's the way it is. But things are more a matter of correspondence than causation. There's a certain correspondence within an already existing system or field, rather than one item causing another.

Rather than only asking how a thing happened, also ask *why* it happened. Asking "how" it happened keeps you limited to physical linearity, asking *why* it happened puts you in touch with the metaphysical reality underlying all things. If you live in a pan-deterministic universe, then there is no "why" and everything happens for no reason, just by coincidence. That's the nihilistic, atheistic, materialists view. This view comes from an inability to view or sense anything outside of what is right in front of you. One then makes conclusions about reality based just on what the eyes see. But in your heart, you know, that's not all of "reality".

When someone has an accident, we usually ask "how" it happened. But that only provides a limited idea of what's going on, only provides the bare mechanics of it: Car A hit Car B. That's *how* it happened. No deeper insight. One level deeper, you go a bit further, into multiple causes or multiple "hows" which is always more useful than the singular "cause" explanation. Was it the kids in the car that distracted the driver? Was it that the streetlight was malfunctioning? Or that the other driver wasn't paying attention either? Or that he was tired? Or that the streets were slippery? Maybe it was some of all of that. And the answer to "why" will show us where all of these incidents actually originate. Then you might see that the driver's life had been stagnating for months and he and his family required a wake-up call.

Yes, for the purpose of common Law, we think in terms of linear cause and effect. But even that usually holds people accountable for the overall energy field they have accumulated and most judges are aware of that.

Things usually start happening long before the actual negative or positive event breaks out. If you know that, you understand non-linear causality. Once something finally manifests, it's the result of many chain reactions and influences which all began in an inner stance, position, attitude, viewpoint or belief. At a higher level of consciousness, your thoughts can manifest quickly. At a lower level, it can take weeks, months or even years before things eventually take their toll on you or reward you. Because it can take a while for things to manifest, it's difficult to uncover the originating thought that eventually led to a certain chain of events. When you ask WHY something happened, you live in the assumption that the originating cause of everything lies more deeply in the spiritual and then you're looking beyond just the obvious and mechanical. Looking only at the linear and mechanical is going to get you confused. You'll start checking the brakes of the car and all kinds of stuff that are not actually related to what really happened from a higher viewpoint. I'm not saying the brakes don't need checking, but I am saying that's not the first thing to check. The first thing to check is yourself. Check yourself before you wreck yourself.

When you have a Goal, ask the "why" question. Why do you want it? And why do you believe you can achieve it? The more reasons you find, the more likely it is to come true. If you look back at your life, you see that a goal coming true usually has multiple causes that go back not only to a "how" but a strong enough reason for wanting it. When I have a goal, I usually employ all kinds of methods, not just one. I want to reach it, no matter what method. Some people become so focused on techniques, but it's more about the right attitude, which could also be called determination or commitment. If you have commitment, any method will work. Tools don't replace the confidence, optimism and authority of the person using them. It's not only about the quality of tools, it's about the person using them. Yesterday's success and yesterday's failure means nothing. Be-cause.

8

Experiencing Time Travel with Consciousness

"There are things that we know and things that are unknown to us. Between them there are doors" – William Blake

In previous books I taught ascending in Levels of Consciousness. Here I'd like to point out that time travel is neither ascending nor descending in consciousness. It is an ability of consciousness. Whether you can time travel or not has no bearing on your level of consciousness or ascent. Nor do any other ESP Skills such as Telepathy, Telekinesis, etc.

Preparation

In this chapter you learn how to focus energy on your ability to time travel. The following exercises are more "warm up" before you use the actual time travel technique.

Breathing in the World

I created this exercise so that you can increase your well-being and the lucidity of your attention. Breathe in the positive, breathe in the negative. Yeah, that's not a misspell. Yoga practitioners know "Breathe in the positive, breathe out the negative". Well, this is breathe in the positive, breathe in the negative. Breathe in Objects. Breathe in Humans. How? Put attention on something and breathe it in. While breathing out, put attention on nothing in particular. Attention on empty. Look at a person, breathe in. De-Focus and breathe out. Look at a worry within and breathe in. De-Focus and gently breathe out. Look at something beautiful and breathe in. Look at nothing and breathe out. Allow breathing to be slow, soft and deep. Instead of lifting the chest, lift primarily the stomach while breathing in. Breathe into your entire Being. While breathing in you imagine breathing everything you are looking at. While breathing out, put awareness on empty. Breathing in the negative means to neutralize it. It is easier to let go of what you "have" and "hold". Breathing in the positive means to welcome it.

Aligning Consciousness with Time Travel

Our Training begins by mentally aligning with the Goal of Time Travel through Consciousness. My definition of Consciousness is that it's composed of attention, thought, perception and energy).

Please practice the following exercises only when and if you enjoy them. An enjoyable or interesting experience, indicates inner alignment.

Your first exercise is to write a report in which you speculate about the Future. Take 30 creative minutes for that. Write about our World as it will be in 50 years, 100 years, 250 years, 500 years, 1000 years and 10 000 years. Examine the development and changes in Technology, Environment, Lifestyle, Politics, Fashion, Music, Entertainment, Communication, Travel, Spirituality and anything else that comes to mind. Include the pleasant and unpleasant.

With this exercise, you are meant to discern or get a feel for the difference between these future-times. You learn to navigate them in Consciousness and stretch awareness to them. In fact, you are already time travelling.

Discerning Imagination and Remote Viewing

Time Travel with Consciousness primarily means to gain such a level of clarity, that you can tell the difference between Imagination – which is an impression created by you – and Remote Viewing – which is an impression received by a location in space or time. It can arrive as a hunch, intuition or the perception of actual events. Remote Viewing allows you to scan any place you like and receive valid Feedback.

Close your eyes for a moment. Notice the chair you are sitting on. Is that perception or imagination?

You could perceive the chair with either mode of consciousness. If you simply put your attention there, with eyes open or closed, you are perceiving. Perception may be vague or clear, but that's what it is. Or you might create a mental replica of the chair or resort to the memory of what it looks like. That's not Perception, that's Thought or Imagination. Knowing the difference is important for remote viewing and time travel. And it also helps to eradicate delusional thinking. If for example, you are jealous of your spouse and think he or she is cheating on you: Is that perception or imagination? It would be hard to tell if you were tense or emotionally upset. You'd have to relax enough to put your attention on something without projection and imagination.

Close your eyes again, and put your attention on the chair.

Now, instead of stretching attention out to the chair, imagine the chair.

You see, one is more of a felt sense of stretching awareness to a place and the other is more of an image created in front of or inside the forehead (or, for some people, elsewhere). See if you can feel the difference between the two.

While you are sitting on it, it's more likely you are perceiving, not imagining. Get up and stand elsewhere in the room. Now close your eyes and first perceive the chair by stretching awareness in that direction. Touch the chair with your awareness. And then, imagine the chair instead, create a mental copy of it.

That's it. You can now return to that chair.

Close your eyes once more and try to perceive the objects around you with eyes closed. This is fairly easy with objects in your immediate surroundings. Stretch awareness outside of that which your senses would be able to see (if your eyes were open). Go beyond the borders of the room and even the House. What do you perceive? Stretch awareness out even more, around the entire area or neighborhood. Are you still dealing with awareness / perception or have you entered the territory of Imagination?

Beginners will have unwittingly and easily switched to imagination. In this exercise, most people can't even tell the difference between perception of something as it is and imagination. It might have been easy with the chair, but may appear difficult with things beyond one's immediate surroundings.

But that difficulty is only an appearance, a habit. We are conditioned and used to only perceiving our surroundings with our eyes, so we *assume* the same applies to the perceptions of our mind. This is very important to understand for those interested in their extrasensory skills.

It's only an assumption. The truth, that may be shocking to some, is that anything you stretch awareness towards, can be perceived. If there is anything that can't be perceived it's because you have put amnesia barriers or blocks on it. But in general, you have access to everything in the Universe. The reason this would be shocking for most people to find out, is because they have spent a lifetime limiting their awareness to only their immediate surroundings.

Remote Viewing is putting awareness somewhere in the absence of thoughts of your own. Whatever impressions you then receive (rather than create) are what is actually there.

The way I have practiced Remote Viewing over the years is on long walks through different towns. I have spent a lifetime travelling the world doing Workshops. After Workshops I usually take a walk. After some time, my mind becomes calm enough to practice remote viewing. I'll be walking toward a street corner and put my awareness to what lies behind it, unseen to the eyes. Then I'll turn the corner and be able to verify with my own eyes. Perceive and Verify – I've repeated this process tens of thousands of times. If you never verify, you will never know whether you are dealing with perception or imagination. But having remote viewed so many times and verified it, I am keenly aware of the difference between the two.

And there is nothing wrong with Imagination. It has its usefulness in other areas, such as improving one's emotional state and attracting preferable outcomes. But for extrasensory perception, you'll want to reduce it.

So that is the practice I am giving you: **Perceive and Verify**. If you do not verify, you might as well be fantasizing. If you enter a new room and there is a wall...stretch awareness through that wall and get a sense of what is behind it. Is it Imagination or Perception? Enter the space behind the wall to see what's really there. Verify. The more often you verify, the better. This will increase your confidence in your extrasensory ability and your "second sight" will improve. It is especially important to verify whenever practical and possible, because with time travels, there is often no possibility to verify. But if you have trained yourself to discern between fantasy and fact, you will have more confidence to determine whether you really travelled to a certain time or not even in instances where you are unable to verify.

ESP is a normal skill of awareness, just like seeing is a normal ability of the eyes. Just because you can see the stuff that is around you, does not mean you have a higher consciousness level or superpowers. So, don't let it get to your head. There is nothing all that amazing about seeing. In fact, some of what you see will actually scare you. But the ability will increase your level of knowledge. You will know more about almost anything. Increased knowledge does not equal increased consciousness or energy. That comes from an elevation in compassion, appreciation and joy, not in an increase of knowledge.

As your knowledge increases, I recommend you also increase your level of consciousness. Having too much knowledge and too much success without increasing your levels of love and compassion, can have adverse effects. People who achieve great knowledge or great success while their Egos are in full bloom, tend to become arrogant, abrasive and even hateful. They become aware of their superior knowledge and view the rest of humanity as stupid and worthless. That is the real danger of increased knowledge. The skill that I just taught you, that of discerning between perception and imagination, has the potential to equip you with unlimited knowledge. With unlimited knowledge can come influence and abundance. And these should only be developed alongside a gentle and kind heart.

Before you continue reading this book, I recommend you spend some time with **perceive & verify**. You might put this book aside for a few days or weeks and instead seek to practice the skill. It is only through this one skill, that extrasensory perception becomes attainable. And it is only through successful experiences with extrasensory perception that the idea of time travel starts feeling reasonable.

Thoughts vs. Perception

One could always use a couple more thought vs. perception exercises.

Close your eyes for a moment and notice the stream of thoughts. 80% of these thoughts are habitual repetition-loops and reactions. Another 15% are probably thoughts that were created by you consciously at one point. And 5% are Intuition or Remote Viewing of things actually happening. Does that mean most people are primarily involved in non-reality? Yes.

What follows are additional exercises to regain clarity. Fully master each step before moving on to the next, even if it takes several minutes, hours, days or even weeks. There is no time pressure, on the contrary, you'll be mastering time. Even if you do not wish to time travel, discerning between Imagination and Perception is helpful for many other skills in life.

Imaginary-Label vs. Pure Awareness

"Before a man studies Zen, to him mountains are mountains and waters are waters; after he gets an insight into the truth of Zen through the instruction of a good master, mountains to him are not mountains and waters are not waters; but after this when he really attains to the abode of rest, mountains are once more mountains and waters are waters." - D.T. Suzuki

Spot an object in the room you are in and observe it for a few moments. In your imagination, create a label or opinion about it and then observe it with this idea in mind. Then once again observe it neutrally, without label or opinion. Repeat this with various opinions and then move on to the next object.

For example, you observe a flower. Then you imagine the flower to be poisonous or dangerous. Look at it that way. Discover things that look dangerous about it. Then cancel this view and simply see the flower as flower. After half a minute of neutral observation, I imagine the flower to be preciously beautiful. I speculate how it could be the rarest of its kind, gifted by a King, a sacred flower, etc. After that, I once again view the flower neutrally, without Imagination. Then I proceed with another object.

After some time, Imagination comes under my control and I can easily discern whether I am Imagining or Perceiving. Sometimes I'll do a few minutes of this, before going to time travel.

Spontaneous Impression

This is to learn about your first spontaneous perception of things, as opposed to your thoughts about them.

Let your gaze flow around the room. If you focus on any object, do so quickly. Don't look at anything longer than half a second to two seconds. You'll notice that if you stay at an object longer, you start forming thoughts about it. So, move your gaze too quickly for your thoughts. Before a thought can arise, your gaze has already moved on. In the split second you are observing an object, awareness is clear, without judgement, interpretation or imagination.

In practicing extrasensory perception (or time travel), you'll sometimes feel the need to reduce distraction or imagination.

In that case, have your gaze move around rather than staying stuck in one place.

Labeling Thoughts with Thought

This is the same exercise as before, but with thoughts.

The mind tends to create automatic chains of association. You think one thing and that automatically brings up another thing - thoughts about thoughts. A mind on automatic can be helpful for daily tasks, but can prevent that you simply perceive what is there. One way to gain control of this, is to take what happens automatically and do it intentionally, by copying each thought that arises. You think "Hm, what do I do now?" and then think it again. You think of a friend and then think of that friend again, intentionally. That's how you gain control of the mind. Please try this right now for about 5 minutes.

If your mind is ever too turbulent to attempt ESP or you simply wish to relax, I recommend a few minutes of "Copying Thoughts".

Another way to regain control of a turbulent mind is to create your own chain of associations (instead of copying the ones that come up). Hold a certain thought, such as "I don't like crowds". Then think "I don't like that thought". And then "That reminds me of my trip to Italy" and then "Well, it was kind of nice". So, you have created your own thoughts about thoughts. You take what your mind normally does automatically and do it intentionally. A few minutes of this will calm the mind and can be done prior to any ESP exercise or any sort of Meditation for that matter.

Another Variation: Observe the stream of thoughts for a few minutes. For every thought that comes up, mentally say "I created that". No matter which thought comes up, think "I created that". Some prefer this variation.

A fourth way to gain control of your thinking: When a thought arises, breathe it in. Hold your breath while holding the thought. While breathing out, let go of the thought.

More on Imagination vs. Remote Viewing

Attention can travel anywhere. Let's say you put it on a faraway restaurant. As before, the question is: Are you perceiving what is there, remembering a restaurant or imagining a restaurant?

In your ESPs and time travels, it's OK to use *some* Imagination as a crutch. It is a primer for actual perception. The trick is, to draw back Imagination, cut it down, the more impressions arise "on their own". First you imagine, then you wait on what arises on its own.

Most people will have a mixture of memory, imagination and extrasensory perception. To separate and discern these is the key that unlocks everything else. But often you'll have to start with some Imagination in order to define Location. Without imagining a place, you cannot tell consciousness which place you wish to receive information from.

Do not use this ability to view remotely, for unethical purposes. If you act as a hidden influence on others, you become susceptible to hidden influences. If for example, you believe you can enter other people's private spaces and spy on them, guess what? It means you also believe you can be spied on without your knowledge. And that means you will be. As you do unto others, so will be done to you.

Time travel is an extreme form of ESP. How clear your time travels are depends on how clear your ESP is. How clear your ESP is, depends on how extensively you have practiced. I realize that some readers won't like to hear that. They'd rather just get abilities without having to practice anything. But when did that ever work? Anything you have ever learned, you have learned through repetition. To learn writing, you have to write a lot. To time travel, you have to time travel a lot.

Look Around

Go with your imagination to a place of your choice. Observe the place for half a minute. Then look to the right and see what is there. Look to the left and perceive what is there. Look upward and perceive what is there. Then turn around and see what's behind you.

This exercise is to overcome the default tendency to see only to the front. We have this tendency because our eyes only look out to the front and most people define their entire world by what they see with their physical eyes. That is ridiculously limited. It is limited in the physical world, where people rarely look upward or around and it is even more of a limitation in the mental world. In the world of mind and spirit, believing you can only look forward, is a habit you picked up while having a body. But it's not true.

As a time traveler, you will be viewing certain scenes from other centuries. While doing so, I recommend you look in all directions instead of just staring straight in front of you in baffled amazement. Looking only out to the front, renders the experience two-dimensional. Looking up and around makes it three-dimensional and you will experience more.

The Higher-Self Viewpoint

All ESP is easier for those who can occupy the Higher Self Viewpoint, which means to increase one's vibration and become silent so that the inner voice can be heard. Instead of seeking to communicate with Higher Self, BE Higher Self. The state is one of effortlessness, non-expectation, relaxation while awake, kindness, openness, interest, curiosity and confidence. For more on this state, see my book "Being Higher Self".

Between Waking and Sleeping

Another way of time travel can be done between waking and sleeping. As the mind is inactive during sleep, extrasensory perception is easy. What is not easy is to keep a part of yourself awake during this time. But if you manage to do that, you can have very intense experiences.

I recall this incident: While falling asleep I told myself that I'd like to travel to the distant future. Right before falling asleep I received strange scenarios that fascinated me greatly. Fascination is an indicator that you are perceiving far outside of your regular, limitations. I knew that I had not yet fallen asleep, but was on the verge. And I knew that the images were a response to my intention.

I found myself standing on a platform, surrounded by turquoise skyscraper-like structures without windows. Nearby there was some fountain that had not been maintained or repaired and was going crazy. The street was flooded and my feet were splashing through the water. This water seemed oddly revitalizing, as if it were more than just water or a different type of water. The skyscrapers felt strangely attractive but I couldn't spot or define why, exactly. I noticed slight oscillations of the objects around me or of my perception, similar to the type of oscillations you have on LSD. I realized it is because I had not entirely stabilized in this time. I took a look around and discovered that the city was empty. Even more fascinating: This "city" was actually quite small. I had assumed it was a city because of the skyscraper-like structures. But it was actually a small village. In just one kilometer distance the desert began and stretched in all directions as far as the eyes could see. I fell asleep.

Yes, targeting a specific time and making an intention while falling asleep, can get you there. As my intention was not specific enough, it took me to a random place. I do not know where and when it was, but I do know it was the distant future to us, because it made very little sense in comparison to what we know. If I had to guess, I'd say it was a probable place around 400 years into the future. The wealth of humanity was so great, that even a small village can afford those beautiful, massive structures.

I first wrote this dream in the 2003 version of the book. Reviewing it again, now in 2020, I realize that the statement "As my intention was not specific enough, it took me to a random place" is not quite true. In retrospect I know that the places one goes are never random and nothing is a coincidence. Things are interconnected in a genius, amazing, brilliant, surprising and thoroughly satisfying way. The Universe is a brilliant work of art. About five or six years ago, I was shown a private display of futuristic architectural models. This was on a Business Trip to the United Arab Emirates. Among the displays there was the idea of technologically self-sustaining, automated villages. I saw the village from my dream there. In my dream I had actually experienced the place that I would be shown 14 years later. While looking at the display, I did not recall the dream. I only saw the connection while translating this part of the 2003 book. That also means me being shown these model cities was no coincidence.

In case you haven't noticed, you have reached a point in the book, where you'd have enough knowledge for plenty of time travel experiments of your own. You could have already started in the second chapter, while I talked about precognitive dreams. And with a little bit of initiative you could have devised time travel exercises of your own, before I even introduce mine. In other words: If you haven't already started, now is the time to experiment on your own.

Time Anchors

Time anchors are important parts of time travel technique. To travel through time, you have to let your mind or subconscious know, where to travel and set an anchor there. Otherwise your trip will seem random. Some people prefer random, they prefer vague parameters, but the mind prefers specifics. I have defined the following three time anchors for this book (I am sure you could come up with others):

a) A self-created timeline with times and place indicators (on a piece of paper or computer file)

b) A picture or book showing events from the past (or in the future)

c) Imagining or Remembering something from the past or future.

Let's experiment with all three.

Create a timeline with various times and places on a piece of paper. Example:

15 00	18 00	2000	2020	2100	2700

Rome	Home	Sydney	Home	Boston	Tokyo

Now determine where you'd like to travel to, mentally or by pointing with your fingers. Close your eyes and think of and feel into that place and time for a minute or more. Let whatever comes up, come up. Much of it could be Imagination, and that's fine at this stage. A part of it may also be real perception, real time travel. When creating a timeline anchor like this, be sure to include places and times that actually interest you. Defining the places that interest you, plays the biggest role in actually reaching those destinations. Just like in daily life, you are more likely to travel to a country if you express an interest to go there.

If you wish to make time travel a regular practice, I recommend you create a more extensive timeline, ranging back thousands of years and going forward thousands or even tens of thousands of years. Put great detail into it. That will prime the subconscious to use it correctly. I know a time traveler who has carved a timeline into a wood table with his own hands and lovingly worked imagery and symbolism into it. He knows that what you put a lot of love and attention into, has a tendency to serve you. It displays a much more sincere desire to time travel than had you just scribbled it on a crumpled or food stained sheet of paper.

Let's try using an image anchor. Get a picture from somewhere. Let's take, for example the Pyramids of Giza. Being iconic, they make for very effective anchors. Look at the picture intensely for a moment. Write the date that you are targeting directly onto the picture. If you cannot write on the picture for some reason, then intend the date mentally. Now look at the same image in your mind's eye. You are using Imagination as your anchor. Define in which time you'd like to perceive what you are seeing. Enter that place in your Imagination. Let any association, image or sensation come up as it wants to.

What do you perceive? Look around. What do you smell? Taste? Hear? See? Feel?

That was the Image Anchor. What you just perceived may have been a mixture of perception and imagination. Perhaps you were curious who built the Pyramids and how they were built. If you travelled 4000 years in the past and they were still standing, then you must travel further. And if you travel 8000 years into the past and they are still standing, then what? Then you might get confused. Don't archeologists say the Pyramids were built 4000 B.C. or something like that? Or was it 2000 B.C.? Then why are they still there when I travel back to 6000 B.C.? In this confusion you might not know whether you are perceiving or imagining. As a result, you'll start thinking the whole practice is pointless and give up altogether.

And that's why it's so important to discern between imagination and direct perception before pursuing time travel. Had that been practiced, it would be clear archeologists are wrong. But if you hadn't trained perception, you wouldn't have the confidence to declare archaeologists wrong and instead doubt in your own sanity.

The timeline and image anchors can also be combined. You'd first make the timeline and then use your mind or fingers to define the "Now" or "Today". Then you'd think of the images on the picture as they appear to you today. You'd think of the Giza Pyramids as they are today. Then you move your finger down the line or in your mind to increasingly earlier times. What did the place look like in the 15th Century? And in the 1st Century? And 6000 B.C.? How about 10 000 B.C.? At what point do the Pyramids disappear? And then, moving forward in time, at what point do they appear? Sure, that's quite advanced, but you do have the ability to see all of that. Or perhaps you'd like to see the Pyramids 10 000 years from now? Are they still there? If not, what is? This skill, once reliably learned and trusted, can provide hours of education and entertainment.

Before we get advanced though, it's important to learn how to define your targeted place and time. To consciousness, everything is taking place at the same time and place. By defining time and place, we learn to separate, to focus and to perceive.

The third anchor type is purely mental. You could also combine it with a physical timeline. Having a scale or timeline can be very helpful for the orientation of the mind. Frankly, the mind is a bit overwhelmed by the fact that time is not actually linear, so giving it that line, calms it down. When its calm, it won't distract you from your time travel work.

A mental anchor means focusing on a certain place or time and staying there for a few minutes. Allow associations and images to arise. Look around. This is the most advanced and direct way to do it, without the need for specific pictures or timelines. This is the way I do it. I simply focus on what I want to perceive and wait for impressions to come up.

But for Beginners anchors are important to perceive anything at all. Some people might perceive a little and then be tempted to say "OK, that's interesting. Cool, I can time travel. What's next?" and then lose interest in the subject. That's a common trick of the mind to keep a person locked in on one particular reality. It is the minds job to keep you focused on one reality, you know. The mind will be quick to find excuses not to pursue time travel. "I know how it works now. It's kind of boring actually. Let's move on to something else". But if it appears boring to you in any way, you have not actually time travelled. What instead happened, is that you were observing mental replicas of things (you were in Imagination-Mode). That's like the difference between looking at a picture of a swimming pool vs jumping into one. Is jumping into one "boring"? Probably not. Is looking at the picture of one for a while, boring? It might be.

Actual time travel is anything but boring. Every trip is a new state, vibe, consciousness, atmosphere, space, realm. And that is deliciously appealing to almost anyone. Any genuine time shift will make you feel quite awake and lucid, as you would when entering brand new spaces.

Wide and Detail Focus

Having arrived in the time of your choice, there are a lot of things you could look at. It's like having stepped into a movie. This can sometimes be overwhelming when the impressions are too many or seem not to match. Understand that it's your decision on how to set the focus of your attention (how to set your mental camera), which things to look at more closely (zoom into) and what to ignore. As long as you don't make any decisions, things might seem a bit fuzzy.

Let's say you have arrived at the Tower of Pisa in the year 1372 (known landmarks make it easier to time travel, because they give you a target to focus on). Now you'll have hundreds of ways to experience it. You could look at it from close up, from above, from inside the Tower. Or you could have less interest in the tower and more attention on the people surrounding it or more focus on the terrain and nature. If you did the exercise earlier, with the Pyramids of Giza, you'll have discovered that the Pyramids were once surrounded by green grass and trees. But I shouldn't be telling you that, because I am front-loading you. Then you'll have an expectation (imagination) rather than pure perception. In time travel it's quite important that you discover things for yourself. It's also a little more difficult to remote perceive when you have acquired too much previous knowledge about a thing, especially when that "knowledge" is false.

So, let's say you're exploring the area around the Tower of Pisa. Possibly you aim for something else and only took Pisa as an approximate landmark. Maybe you wish to locate a certain House in the area belonging to your ancestors, investigate the fashion of that era or check the climate in those times. Maybe it's a bookshop in old Pisa you are looking for. There are no rules about what you should focus on. Decide, based on what interests you. Simply know that, whatever it is you explore, will have some effect on your emotional state and experience in your regular time and daily life. It's not possible to have deep experiences and return without being influenced. Look at something and it looks back at you. It is therefore advisable to time travel consciously, not only for pure entertainment. Or to at least have a specific goal in mind or intend for a certain result or piece of knowledge.

More on Imagination vs. Perception

Imagination can be seen as a Bridge to actual perception. If Imaginary things come up while you are in perception-mode, that's fine. Perception of reality often arises after imaginary thoughts were let go of. What that means is if there were no imaginary impressions (anchors), there may also be no reality-perceptions that replace them. In this way, imagination supports perception.

As soon as Imagination has served as an anchor or aimer, roll it back. Imagination has served its purpose and you are now ready for receiving "flashes" of the time you targeted. These really do feel different than normal imagery, but you have to experience this yourself to understand the difference. The more you practice, the longer the "flashes" last, until they are no longer just flashes but full-length feature films.

In regards to Imagination, Parallel Universe travel is different from past or future travel. Past or Future travel assumes a number of facts as they exist on your particular timeline. There is room for the interpretation of what these facts mean, but the facts remain the facts. If the Giza Pyramids where built more than 12 000 years ago, before the flood, then that's a fact, regardless of what archaeologists imagine. Parallel Universe travel, however, relies on Imagination a bit more. Imagination is in fact the tool with which to gain information from other Universes. Imagination itself might very well be perception of parallel universes. When accessing parallel universes, the goal is therefore not to cut out imagination entirely, but moderate its use.

Use all of your Senses

Whether you are imagining or perceiving – your experience is not limited to what you see. It's amazing how many people have to be reminded of the simple fact. Most of their attention is used on visuals. But you can also experience a place, event or person by hearing it, smelling, tasting or feeling emotional vibration. You are able to turn up the volume, intensity color, get a sense of atmosphere and feeling – this will give you a much clearer idea of what's going on than just relying on visuals. You may be at the tower of Pisa.

But frankly, it didn't look all that different than it looks today. The main thing happening is the "vibe" of the place, the "atmosphere". You'll find it to be very different to the vibe you have today. You see, the truth of the matter – and one of the greatest secrets of the Universe – is that you are not actually time travelling, as time does not exist. You are travelling into different vibratory frequencies.

Technique for Experiencing Parallel Timelines

You've already learned the raw material of this technique in the Parallel Worlds Meditation a few chapters back. If you have practiced that Meditation, you already understand how to perceive parallel worlds. Here's a summary of that technique:

1. Remember a real situation in your personal past
2. Remember a decision that you made back then
3. In your Imagination, decide differently than you decided and follow the timeline of events as they would presumably play out.

An example:

1. You remember a situation your mother had a few years ago. You spend a minute or more in that memory.
2. You recall a decision she made back then that changed her life.

3. Imagine her making another decision and follow the possible chain of events in her life, on this new timeline.

Another Example:

`1. You remember the attack on the World Trade Center in 2001.

2. The Decision was to go ahead with the attack and thereby change the Course of History.

3. Imagine that it had been decided not to stage the attack. Follow the Course of events. What might be different? How would politics and History develop from that point forward?

The parallel-timelines technique is not only useful for this book. By using it you become aware of how deeply your decisions determine the Course of your life. And that has a positive effect on you in general.

That's the rough idea we are now going to look at more deeply:

Expansion of the Parallel World Technique

1. Become aware of an important decision that you could make today or in the next days.
2. Imagine you make a decision for one path and follow the possible consequences in your imagination
3. Imagine you make a decision for another path and follow the possible consequences in your imagination.

This doubles as a technique for decision making. If you don't wish to do this mentally, you can draw a few lines or tracks beside each other on a piece of paper. At the beginning of one of the tracks you put yourself and at the beginning of other tracks you write down one of the decisions you could make, including the decision not to decide. Follow each parallel timeline to its probable long-term consequences.

Something More Intense

Imagine there are several versions of you, already living on different timelines. If one decision = 1 timeline-switch, then one Identity = 100 timeline-switches. That means, in 100 decisions or tracks from now, you're another person. Someone that has made so many decisions differently, that he become someone else (even though that person still has similarity to you in genetic makeup and possibly in level of consciousness).

1. Imagine another _____ (insert your name) – Identity. There are latent and potential parts of you, other versions of you inside, waiting to come out. Which might those be? Could it be a parallel world version of you? What are talents you suspect but haven't yet tried?

2. Mentally or in Writing, follow the life of this other version of you. This version of you who decided hundreds of things differently.

3. If you want, establish communication to this other version of you.

Note: The longer you focus on this other version of you, the more similar your decisions become to his or hers and then your tracks start merging int that direction. If you don't mind that, then keep focusing.

After you have become accustomed to this technique, there are some interesting questions to ponder:

1. Which deeper motivation is behind most of the decisions that you or another version of you made? Is it love, fear, desire or aversion?
2. Would the Highest Version of you have made these decisions?
3. What would happen in your life if you always made decisions from the perspective of the highest version of you?

Method for Experiencing the Past

We've finally arrived at the core of the book – the time travel technique. Here's a little secret: Most techniques and methods are entirely dependent on belief and repetition. If you believe something works and repeat it several times (for example once a day for a whole month), it starts working, no matter what it is. An example: I recall an incident where an acquaintance of mine got the most bizarre recommendations to heal a serious illness. He hadn't been able to have it healed anywhere. I mocked the practice. I didn't believe in it. He believed. He repeated it faithfully for months. The illness healed.

The time travel technique shared here is a tool, a construct, an anchor. It is something to hold on to, so you can believe and repeat. But ultimately, it's not about the tools, it's about the worker using the tools. If there is a bad worker, then none of the tools work. But if the worker is good, then he or she could make any nonsense work. Not because of how awesome the tools are, but how awesome the worker is. I am going to assume you are an average worker and give you tools that are as clean and simple as possible. How many repetitions will you need to have real and a reliable experience of time travel? That depends on who is asking. Fortunately, repetition is only required when one is starting out. Once a behavior is "programmed", it gains a life of its own and becomes easier. This really applies to any skill.

I will now present the technique for perceiving the past.

1. Take on the viewpoint of higher Self (relaxed, neutral, humorous, compassionate)
2. Locate an anchor in the past

You require a point of orientation in the past, that you can anchor to. This can be either

a) *a timeline you draw on a piece of paper, including times (centuries, days, years, depending on scope) and places.*
b) *An image or book about an event from the past*
c) *Imagine or Remember a point in the past*

3. In your mind, create a Bubble that contains the impressions of this time-span. A time-span can, for example, be 1932 to 1933 or 1775 to 1777. You might already be perceiving things at this point, or not.

4. Put yourself (consciousness, awareness, being, feeling) into the Bubble. Wait for impressions that come up by themselves (having learned to discern between imagination and perception).

5. Follow the flashes or impressions that interest you the most. If an impression disappears too quickly, you can restore it with the help of imagination. Once its restored release imagination again and allow for other "flashes" to appear.

When you are ready to leave the Bubble and return back to your own time, tell yourself that this is the time-span so-and-so (insert the year you were in). It's important that you name it as you defined it. So, if you defined it as 1932 to 1933 in Chicago you say "*That's* the time span 1932 to 1933 in Chicago". Doing so takes you back to a viewpoint outside of the bubble. If you are a beginner it may seem like this doesn't matter. It may seem like all you have to do is open your eyes and you are back home. But as your experience becomes more intense, you'll want to use this specific technique of naming-the-time, to get out of it. Realize that the Bubble is neither the NOW or YOU. Let go of it and open your eyes.

In the Members-Section of my website at www.realitycreation.org I have a guided audio version of the Time Travel Technique and several other exercises from this book.

What follows are examples from my own experience with the time travel technique. Read them before trying it out yourself.

1. I meditate for five minutes to put myself into the viewpoint of higher self.
2. On a piece of paper, I have made a timeline 1950 to 2020. In 1955 I inserted the place "Times Square, New York".
3. I put my finger on that point and create a Bubble that contains the year 1955 and Times Square, NY. I release the hand from the piece of paper and focus on the empty space inside the bubble.
4. I enter the bubble. Imaginings arise, I dissolve them. Blackness comes up (which is also Imagination) and I dissolve it. Distractions come up; I dissolve them. All that's left is light emptiness. I wait.

After about 10 minutes I get the first impressions. Where do they come from? Mass consciousness? The akashic chronicles?

I realize I am not remembering them, as the images are not in black and white. If they were in black and white, I'd know I'm remembering 1950s New York from pictures or movies. I see the lights of Manhattan. I put my attention down on the street, as I seem to be hovering somewhere above. I receive images of how people were dressed in the 50s, but I recognize they are probably imagination, so I let go of them and wait.

5. Finally, real impressions arise. A Limo. A lady carrying a Christmas gift. High buildings. For unknown reasons, I'm pulled to a building I don't know (the subconscious seems to find things relevant, even if we don't consciously know why they are relevant). It's a group of men sitting around a table. I can tell it's an important, far-reaching meeting, otherwise I wouldn't have been pulled there. Distracting images arise again (almost all distractions are things I have read, heard or seen before). I delete them and wait. Suddenly other imagery of the city comes up. I don't necessarily recognize times square, but that could be because of the angle from which I am viewing or because it has changed so much since then. Looking it up later for verification, I see I had not recognized it because it's centerpiece at the address "Times Square 1" that I was "expecting", was not yet well defined in those days.

I intend to be back in the room. I'm back. I hear one of the men saying "Is there someone in this room with us?" I am surprised that he can intuitively feel my presence. Not only surprised, also embarrassed, as if I have been found out. I leave the place. I'm magnetically pulled toward Broadway. It's all quite amazing. I feel like I wouldn't mind staying here. The images are now more intense, more real, I feel as if I am really present. So much so, that I might be seen by the people there. There is a crowd of people in front of the entrance of a building. It's some event. I am there. I can now clearly feel that if I were to increase the degree of intensity, would start perceiving me. Right now, I might look like a Ghost to them. I choose to break off for now, it's been intense enough for today.

6. I name the Bubble "New York 1955" and then find myself outside of it. I look at the images inside the Bubble for a few seconds. Imagination is once again mixing with them. I turn the Bubble off, as I would turn off a TV and am left touched and astonished by the experience.

Another Example:

1. I shift my viewpoint to that of higher self. With slow and deep stomach breathing I maintain this level.

2. I remember my imagined ideas of "Ancient Egypt". I am interested in whether the Great Pyramids were built by humans or other beings and what Technology was used. I imagine the Pyramid.

3. I create a Bubble and determine it contains the time-span in which the Pyramids were built. That's because I don't know when that was, but wish to find out.

4. I consciously let go of Memory and Images and get an open mind. The empty Bubble does not feel empty at all. It feels deep and mysterious and I know it is about to reveal something to me that not many people know. It feels like I am about to enter forbidden terrain. I enter the Bubble feeling adventurous. I feel like I am sucked into a vortex. No imaginary stuff comes up, fortunately, only darkness for now. I can feel intuitively that I am in a time that is clearly older than 4000 to 6000 years. It feels more like 12 000 to 20 000 years ago. And still darkness. Suddenly imaginary material does show up. Nonsense I saw in the movie "Stargate" or read in books on Ancient Aliens. I recognize them as imagined and remembered and let go of them all. Imaginary things are much weaker than perceptions of physical realities. In this darkness a sound comes up. I recognize the sound as remote perception. The

sound creates a rush of energy through my spine, like a deep electronic horn, monotonous and mysterious. Were the Pyramids assembled with some kind of sound? Possibly! The information doesn't make any sense to the mind. Nor is it anything I desired to hear. But I delete my skepticism and simply perceive. There is a lot more darkness in this session than in others, almost as if this particular place and time is full of veils and covers. Suddenly I see the completed Pyramid in front of me. It is shining in Gold. The sound fades away. The Pyramid looks different than I had imagined or know from my native time. Why is it Gold? I don't know. It also has a golden cap that is distinct from the rest of the Pyramid. The atmosphere and climate are much different than I expected. At one point, the sky is strangely orange-yellow, as if fires have been raging all day. Nor do I understand why the Pyramid appears to be bigger than the one we know. Is this not the same Pyramid? Plants and trees are growing around it, unlike the desert it is today. At another time I saw lush Jungle growing around it, but not at this time. I am absolutely pleased with my state because I'm able to keep a stable view of this time. Suddenly I realize the Pyramid is not bigger than the one in my native time, but it's not half buried in sand. Then I saw normal looking humans as well as incredibly large looking humans. Are those giants? Did giants build the Pyramids?

What happened after, I won't say because I'd like to encourage people to make their own explorations. Otherwise, whatever I write here will turn into distractions you experience while attempting to time travel.

These were two examples of time travel, but there are many different ways your personal experience could go. Don't let my examples limit you in any way. This happens to be the structure I use and the way I do it, you might choose to do it differently. It's really a matter of intent, definition and awareness and it doesn't matter so much what structure you put that into.

There is one step missing in both examples: Verification.

If you want to generate more success, you'll want to verify at least some of what you perceive. The two examples above are not easy to verify. There are things that can be verified by reading History books or newspaper archives or by researching in the Internet. But in the case of the Pyramids, much knowledge was lost after the Great Flood, and also manipulated thereafter, so factual verification is hard to come by.

I still recommend you do not take too many trips without verification. If you do so, you will lose track of what's real and easily be deceived. If you verify at least 20% of your time travels, you are being professional and paving the way for increased clarity and reality.

One of the ways I verify time travels is by getting a book that describes or shows what it looked like at a certain place and time. Before I look into the book, I travel there in consciousness. Then I check whether perception and reality match. Sometimes I purchase the book after the trip so that I make sure I am taking a trip through time rather than a trip to the book. Because I am interested in subjects that can't be verified, I make sure to add verifiable exercises as buffer-sessions in between the ones that really interest me.

Having your extrasensory perceptions confirmed and verified is a moment of power. It's the moment the non-physical merges with the physical, the mystery merges with the pragmatic. Proof is empowering. It makes all the difference between a skilled time traveler and a delusional kook. Proof strengthens your confidence and also your extrasensory ability. And that doesn't mean having to prove it to others. You have nothing to prove to others. But you do need to prove it to yourself.

It's now time to practice the Technique for Experiencing the Past. I recommend you use it at least 5 times on different times and places before reading on.

Success Rates

Having used this technique and the following, for a few years, in live seminars with people, these are the success rates I have had so far:

15% report great success. They intensely experienced the place as if they were present there AND were able to verify facts about it.

25% report success and intense experiences and were partially able to verify facts.

50% report intense perceptions and experiences that they were not able to verify.

80% report that the techniques led to more intense lucid dreams that provided information about past and future.

10% report to make no progress with the techniques. The ability is simply blocked for them, but I don't know why. I'd recommend emotional clearing around the subject.

Almost nobody reports of any healing effects. This manner of time travel is less of a healing method and more of a means of exploration and learning. It is not to be mistaken with past life regression. Past life regression assumes that the "you" that you are now, has lived in another time and place and that you can access memories of those past "yous". Time Travel extends well beyond that, saying that you can access any place and time, anywhere, no matter whether "you" have been there before or not. Why? Because consciousness is not limited to a particular body, place or time.

Method for Experiencing the Future

The technique for experiencing the future is the same as the time travel technique for experiencing the past.

1. Enter the Viewpoint of Higher Self
2. Choose an Anchor in the Future

This is a point of orientation in the future. It could be one of these three things:

a) A timeline on a piece of paper, with times and places.
b) An image or book about a possible event in the future.
c) An imagined idea about something in the future.

3. Create a Bubble that contains the impressions of the time-span. You might already perceive something within the Bubble, or not.
4. Go into the bubble and reduce Imagination. Wait on impressions that come up on their own (discerning between Imagination and Perception).
5. Follow the impressions that interest you the most. Experience.
6. To leave that Bubble, name it as the time-span you defined. Your viewpoint will shift from inside to outside.
7. Let Go, stop feeding it attention and open your eyes.

What follows is an example of one of my own time trips to the future. This example however, is not typical, it was special.

1. After a few rounds of conscious breathing I am the Higher Self Viewpoint.

2. My anchor is a dream I recently had. I dreamed of being in a very large, futuristic city, similar to those shown in sci-fi – very high-tech, lots of steel, glass, concrete and flying cars. I put my focus and love on this memory-snippet from the dream.

3. I create a Bubble in which everything I know about the city, is contained. I project myself into the Bubble and look around. Even just the Imagining is already beautiful, so I enjoy the imaginary space for a few minutes. Then I roll back Imagination to zero and wait what returns from this image I sent out.

4. I wait for a while, drift into half sleep. I'm pleasantly surprised when flashes of this place come up. It's another planet and that planet is covered with this city. It's enormous, unearthly. It's depth, height, length, width and volume are vaster than anything I've ever seen. If humans were to build this it would take a thousand years, at our current level. The city not only covers the entire surface of the Planet, it also covers its interior. Perhaps the entire Planet is

artificially constructed city-scape. It is more enormous than in my dream and also more amazing than in any movie I have seen. I am intuitively made to understand that the people living here are human-like, a split-off civilization from normal humans. They have chosen to live on a cityscape that has no green or nature. It's almost as if they were nature-phobic. Overwhelmed by the glistening lights, I switch on Imagination for a moment, to gain some distance (overwhelm is not uncommon, as we are dealing with vastly different frequencies than we are used to). I imagine I move away from the planet and wait. A few seconds later, flash-like impressions arise, of the planet in some distance. As these are somewhat vague, I decide to end the exercise. I name the Bubble "time span 3000 to 3300 A.C." and release attention from it.

I recommend you now practice future time travel at least five times before reading on. Practice makes perfect. It is quite possible that you perceive nothing at all initially. Most people are so deeply asleep, spiritually speaking, they don't even believe in their ESP ability. Even if they do, many are weak-willed and tired. For the majority it will take some practice, and five repetitions of each technique is the least one could do to get started. Those who are used to meditation-type disciplines will have no problem gaining results right away.

Refining Your Time Travel Skills

Normally you Imagine a time, then you roll back Imagination and wait for impressions that come up on their own. If none arise after some time, then return to Imagination and let go of imagining once again.

Imagine,

Let Go,

Imagine,

Let Go,

Imagine,

Let Go.

This is like using Imagination to coax, goad or lure ESP to come out of hiding.

Beginners will frequently only experience "flashes" for some time. The trick is to find entry to these flashes so it becomes an experience as if you were really there. That's vastly different from dream or image. Eventually flashes become longer and more detailed. This happens over time and with practice. It helps to go into deeper relaxation, while staying awake. The state you have right before falling asleep, causes the flashes to move by more slowly so that you can attempt to "enter" them, to merge consciousness with them. Again, people with experience in altered states of consciousness, will have an easier time with all of this.

I too experience just brief flashes most of the time. But when I'm very deliberate about time travel, it goes beyond that so that I am fully present in another time. I can then see everything clearly, I can hear, taste, smell, feel, etc. In rare cases I can even walk around in that time and interact with the people. I am then a complete time traveler. The reason these cases are rare is our own responsibility. Often, they are overwhelming. When I get that deeply into another time, the shift in energy or vibration is so strong it effects my daily life in my native time. Having too many such experiences is not necessarily that desirable, as you might find out on your own. There is an upside and downside to anything and that includes time travel. If you go deep and spend a lot of time in another time, expect this to affect your mood and what you experience back in your native time. I'll give a specific example:

There was a time I travelled back to the pre-flood days of Atlantis. At around the same time, I created a website around the topic and wrote two books on it. On the time jumps, I experienced a lot of weirdness and saw a lot of things I had rather not seen. My prejudice was that all would be fair and beautiful, as I had been told in countless new age books. But those pre-flood times were actually quite rough. No, more than rough: Horrific. That's why Atlantis was destroyed in the first place. It didn't' just sink for no reason. The ruling elite of Atlantis was depraved. So, when people nowadays tell me they wish to "restore the glory of Atlantis" on Earth, I ask myself: What exactly do they want to restore? I don't want to restore that. Maybe they want to restore the glory of Atlantis as it was much longer ago, not the fallen Atlantis shortly as it was before the flood. In any case, all these time trips brought up strange events in my daily life. I was contacted people claiming to be U.S. Military Personnel. They booked coaching-sessions with me just to ask questions about Atlantis. I was contacted by other spook-type people that talked to me in a slightly threatening tone.

I was asked things such as *"Has anyone else contacted you about this?"* – *"Have you been contacted by Government people?"* – *"Have you told anyone about this?"* I realized these people took the topic a bit too seriously. At one point the website got hacked and all the data deleted. So, I re-wrote and re-pasted all the content into the website. Then it got attacked again and all the data removed. So, I decided to just quit the whole project. But these events very much matched the stressful vibe I felt when visiting Atlantis itself. I was bringing this vibe back from the trips and it was mixing with my daily life, attracting all sorts of weird people. That's how I quit time travelling there and quit researching it. After I quit, the weirdness disappeared and all went back to friendliness.

I'll contrast that with a positive example: I had been exploring a particular place and group of people about 200 years in the future. This group of people was having a very positive impact on society with something we might call "mobile houses". The idea is that you can easily relocate your

House anywhere you like, if it doesn't impede on others. In our native time, we have the idea of mobile homes, but these are tiny contraptions that we can ride on highways, compared to these mobile houses. Houses 200 years from now, are mostly made from a material we don't even know. It's hard and light at the same time. It's light enough to be flown anywhere – hence mobile house. And hard enough to be completely stable and withstand any sort of impact. I had to visit this group and place several times to understand what exactly their Business was. The group was not involved in making or transporting these houses, they were involved in *creating* land. Not buying or selling already existing land, but creating land that did not yet exist. A person who wished to relocate their house could either buy land from the Government, from a private owner or they could have this group of people create land, in accordance with the law. Thus, they would design islands, cliffs, landscapes, towns and villages and bring them into existence.

Visiting this time positively affected my daily life in native time. During those trips there were two incidents in which I was very "lucky" with real estate and property. I sold a lot of land to a family who wanted to build a house and I sold it for twice the amount that I originally wanted. And I purchased a house in an area that would see a massive uptick in house prices over the next years because Government suddenly decided they would relocate a harbor and port nearby.

On Black-screens: I can't prove it, but in some places, there appear to be blackouts, fog, blocks or protective walls, similar to Google Earth blurring out places someone doesn't want you to see. These seem to be an effort to keep certain things private and manage what others see. Either it's my own subconscious blurring out certain realities, or there is some kind of reality-editing going on from another realm. Perhaps there are universal privacy rules. In these rare cases, I usually practice restraint and back off. I have nonetheless tried to break through these barriers on some occasions. I've tried to point imagination to what might lie beyond these screens, similar to projecting awareness through the walls of the room I am in. Sometimes that works to deliver information, sometimes it doesn't. Another method I've used is to replicate the fog or wall and put it there myself and then remove it. I repeat this several times and it sometimes creates results in the form of sudden flashes or views of what's behind the screen. My intuitive sense about these time screens is that not all things are appropriate for the development of a person. They may not be ready to experience or capable of processing certain information, and so these things are more difficult to access. But I also believe that if I decide to see and know anyway, it's still my choice. The blocks are merely the question "Are you sure you want to see? Are you really ready?" So far none of my insights after breaking through these walls were pleasant or desirable, so in most cases I don't bother breaking through them. There is a whole infinite Universe of stuff to discover, and no need to insist to see the unpleasant.

Method for Experiencing the History of an Object, Place or Person

This is a method of psychometry.

1. Take an object into your hands and examine it from all sides.
2. Put yourself inside the object. Merge your consciousness with it. Be the Object.
3. Once you "are" the object, remember your past or future. Allow impressions to arise (do not force them).

Alternatives to Step 3:

- Once you "are" the Object, ask: Where or What were you 100 years ago?" or "What were you in 100 years?" (as if the future had already happened). Or simply let whatever comes up, come up, without defining a time.

Handling Doubts

If there are any blocks to your time travel at all, then they lie in your lack of confidence. In this case, handle your doubts so that you discover conscious and subconscious thoughts that are in your way. The following method is taken from my book "*The Reality Creation Technique*". In the left column on a piece of paper, you state your intention. In the right column you state doubts, objections, inner resistances, counter-intentions, disbelief, etc. In the third column you put extended subconscious thoughts that are uncovered through the question "How can you prove this statement is true?" (You asked this two the statement in the second column).

Here's an example to make the exercise clearer:

INTENTION	OBJECTION	PROOF
I am a time traveler	Nonsense. There is no such thing.	If there were, science and the media would have said so.
I am a time traveler	I'm really a dreamer to fall for this nonsense.	They used to call me an airhead in school.
I am a time traveler	I wish.	Every ad promises more than it keeps.
I am a time traveler	I guess in principle it could work, but I don't know how	I've tried the techniques here but they didn't work.
I am a time traveler	Maybe someday.	Skills take forever to learn. It took me years of daily

		practice to learn to play the guitar the way I do.
I am a time traveler	Maybe, but its loads of work. I don't see the point.	All people have to work before they are rewarded.
I am a time traveler	I don't have time to practice.	Things take time and practice

I am a time traveler	Garbage. This book is Garbage. I can't believe I'm this naïve.	The author provides zero references or proof for his own skill.
I am a time traveler	Wow. That would be great.	I could really show off my skill.
I am a time traveler	Why is it actually so difficult for me? That's ridiculous.	It seems easy to the author.
I am a time traveler	Maybe this stuff is dangerous.	There are people in a psychiatry talking like this.
I am a time traveler	Time doesn't even exist, so why is	That's true. All I know is the now.

	time travel relevant at all?	
I am a time traveler	I'm starting to believe it.	Repeat it often enough and you start to believe it.
I am a time traveler	This is getting boring.	When something is boring, it means it doesn't really interest me.
I am a time traveler	I have no inner reaction or objection right now.	My mind is empty.

I am a time traveler	What does it actually mean to time travel in consciousness? What is consciousness?	?
I am a time traveler	Whatever	Dunno
I am a time traveler	I'll try it right after this. We'll see if it works.	Gotta verify.

I am a time traveler	Yeah, need to try it right now.	If I try, I will know.
I am a time traveler	I can barely lose weight or pay my bills. How am I supposed to time travel?	The author recommends I be my "higher self" before I time travel.
I am a time traveler	So what? Again: What's the point?	If there's no benefit, it shouldn't be done.
I am a time traveler	I'll do my best.	Can't do more.
I am a time traveler	If I wait for something to come up, nothing comes up.	Unless I imagine something to come up.

I am a time traveler	Too many distractions. I need to learn to meditate.	I know that.
I am a time traveler	Somehow this exercise isn't working either, I keep having the same thoughts.	?

I am a time traveler	Maybe so. Many smart people say that time only exists as a construct of the mind.	I've read that many times.
I am a time traveler	I'm feeling sad now.	There is a heaviness in my chest.
I am a time traveler	When is this exercise over finally?	Thoughts just keep coming up.
I am a time traveler	OK, so I am.	I've noticed a few time anomalies in my life.
I am a time traveler	I'm a time traveler. Alright. Why not.	If I really want that, I guess I could be that.
I am a time traveler	I am a time traveler.	I am a time traveler

That's an example of what the exercise could look like. It can be done in writing or verbally, provided that you keep repeating the original intention (in the left bracket) to solidify it. Anything other than "I am a time traveler" is seen as an objection. You do it until your mind is empty and no spontaneous objections come up or you fully feel the reality of your intention and fully believe in it. No second guessing, no self-monitoring, no tension, simply "I am a time traveler".

Creating Your Own Time Travel Methods

If you have had some positive experiences with my methods, I recommend you develop some of your own. Why? Because things that come from you, work better for you. Second-hand knowledge is great but your inner knowledge is better.

Your inner self led you to this book because it wants you to explore more.

My intention was to present time-travel methods that could work for anyone. That doesn't mean one couldn't find something better.

Between Waking and Sleeping

Some years ago, I had a phase in which I felt fatigued. I was burned out from excessive work. The tiredness was my body calling me to rest and regenerate. Instead of getting agitated about my tiredness or taking medication or coffee or whatever, I used this phase of sleepiness for ESP and Lucid Dreaming research. All these delicious experiences can be found in between waking and sleeping. While it was cold outside, the streets covered in ice, rain and snow, I retreated, darkened the room and explored. My tiredness opened the window to other worlds. My laziness was rediscovered as alpha, theta and delta brainwave states. Throughout approximately four weeks I spent a lot of time taking naps and drifting in and out of sleep. It is during this time that I discovered the most about the subconscious and its endless dreamscapes, out of body experiences and travelling through time. Often it would be enough to give myself a command, close my eyes, and I'd be there. These are some commands I gave myself while drifting into half-sleep:

"Show me this place in 30 years"

This command took me into a semi-lucid dream. It was obviously the same place, but it looked very different. Instead of looking out into fields and woods, I saw suburban sprawl. The cars looked different. The building I lived in, was still there, but it no longer looked new but rather used up and its white had turned into gray. I then fell asleep.

"Show me this place in the year 1450"

After deeply relaxing, all kinds of images and thoughts came up. Eventually I forgot that I had given a time travel command. It was only when images of woods arose that I remembered the command. The only thing existing here in 1450 were dense and wild woods. There was obviously no Ranger tending to the place. It all looked a bit wilder than I had imagined the distant past to look. I saw the image blurred but knew for certain it was a response to my command. I became more interested and decided to lift up into the air in order to possibly see a city I suspected already existed back then. For some reason, my will wasn't strong enough at the time and I somehow fell asleep. Later I did some online research, to verify what I had seen. Sure enough, there was no known settlement or village in the area at the time. I found that there must have been resting places for horses nearby, but all I had seen is dense forest.

As you can see here, my time travel technique is often as simple as giving a command of where I want to go, and then drifting off into the state between waking and sleeping. Sometimes it really is as simple as that.

Futures are Probabilities

Don't be too alarmed at dystopian scenarios or nuclear explosions in the future. That doesn't necessary mean it's going to happen. You are seeing probabilities based on current trends. From the now-perspective, the future is not yet written. View the same place again in a better mood and you might witness something else. Sometimes your perceptions are not clear, they mix with your fears (which is not perceiving, it's imagining). It is only when you see a disaster repeatedly and in increased intensity, that the probability of it really happening increases. In this case, maybe it's time to plan a relocation. The future is not fixed and can be changed at any time, individually and collectively.

On-Site Perception

At interesting places such as Castles, a Lakeside, a town center or a monument, one might ask what the place looked like long ago or will look like in the distant future. That's good practice for time and perception flexibility. I sometimes do that and let my eyes blur a little so that I can exit the present. If there are intense emotions connected to a place you sometimes don't have to do anything, you'll perceive other times whether you like it or not. Such places are considered "haunted". Sometimes the information is not received in flashes but rather feelings.

Movies as Anchors

Movies can be used as Anchors. The movie takes the role Imagination would normally have. The movie plays at a certain time and place and you let yourself be influenced by that. Afterwards, you close your eyes and target that place as a time-travel destination. You could ask yourself trigger questions such as "Was it like in the film or was it different?" – "In which way was it different"

You may have already used this method in childhood. Don't you remember? After watching a movie, you went to bed and thought about it for a while. And then you imagined being at the place. You may have identified with or fallen in love with one of the characters. And then your "dreams" took you there.

Lucid Dreaming

Another way to time travel is through lucid dreaming. I have already provided a manual for lucid dreaming in my book titled "Being Higher Self" so I will not repeat myself here. If you desire to explore this avenue, please refer to that book. Suffice it to say that time travel in lucid dreams is very easy. Learning lucid dreaming itself is not that easy. But once you know it, there is no limit to where you can go.

Refreshing Your Interest in Time Travel

This section is to be read months or years after finishing the book. Bookmark it for later review.

Part 1

I have written this section for you to refresh your interest in and alignment with time travel as a regular part of your life. The questions and statements that follow, trigger inspiration.

1. If you were to write a book about time travel yourself, what exercise would you invent to perceive other times?
2. Which specific places and times would you like to visit when you are able to?
3. What else would you like to know about time travel?
4. What would you like to feel about time travel?
5. What would like to do toward time travel?
6. Who would you like to be regarding time travel?
7. Do you know someone else who is interested in this and if so, would you like to talk to that person?
8. Remember a time in which time travel strongly interested you.
9. Remember a time you believed time travel is possible.
10. Remember a time someone else thought time travel is not possible.
11. What do you know for certain about time?
12. Is your answer to the last question really true?

Part 2

You know how quickly books are forgotten and then discarded on some shelf or some eBook-readers archive? After a year, take this book back out and go through the following process. You might see things differently at different times of your life. You might see time travel more clearly or have higher ability at another time. These questions will re-ignite the time traveler in you.

1. Name 10 places where you are not
2. Name 10 places where you'd like to be
3. Name 10 places where no human has presumably ever been.
4. Name 5 people of which you know they are interested in time travel
5. Name 5 people of which you know they are not interested in time travel
6. Name 5 non-human lifeforms (fictitious or real, no animals and plants), that are known to you.
7. Name 5 reasons you are not good at time travelling
8. Name 5 reasons others are not good at time travelling.
9. Name 5 reasons why you are good at time travelling.
10. Name 5 reasons why others are good at time travelling.
11. Name 3 reasons why you don't want to time travel.
12. Name 3 reasons why others don't want to time travel.
13. Name 3 reasons why you want to time travel.
14. Name 3 reasons why others want to time travel.

15. Name 10 things you are grateful for and right after that, 3 reasons why you are grateful for time travel.
16. Which disadvantages could time travel have?
17. Which advantages could time travel have?
18. What is one item from this book, that didn't work?
19. What is one item from this book that did work?
20. How could time travel increase your knowledge?
21. How could time travel increase your finances?
22. How could time travel increase your sexuality?
23. How could time travel increase your perception?
24. How could time travel increase your Energy?
25. How could time travel increase your Fascination?
26. How could time travel increase your Courage?
27. How could time travel increase your Confidence?
28. How could time travel increase your Time?
29. What do you feel is true about time travel?
30. What do you feel is untrue about time travel?
31. What do you feel is true about time travel that others think is untrue?
32. What do you think is untrue about time travel that others think is true?
33. What do you know about time travel with absolute certainty? Name 10 things.
34. What could you teach others about time travel that would help them experience it?
35. Are you awake or dreaming?
36. Name 10 reasons why your personal ability to time travel is important for you and others.

37. What time is it?

After completing the process, have another look at your answers for any insights, change of attitude or conclusions.

9

Strange Synchronicity

Synchronicity

Perhaps the best evidence we have that time is not fixed but rather intermixed is the phenomenon of Synchronicity. I have described Synchronicity elsewhere; here I will provide a few examples of it as it relates to time travel. What follows are only a few selections. These are not the exception, they are the norm for anyone who cares to look. The world would be very surprised to learn how interconnected everything is.

The Sinking of the Titanic

In the year 1898 the author Morgan Robertson wrote a novel called "The Wreck of the Titan", that quite accurately predicted what would happen 14 years later with the Sinking of the Titanic.

- Both the fictitious Titan and the Titanic were triple-screwed British passenger liners with a capacity of 3000 and a top speed of 24 knots.
- Both were considered unsinkable and both carried too few lifeboats.
- Both sank in April in the North Atlantic after colliding with an iceberg on the forward starboard side.
- Both hit the iceberg due to excessive speed.
- Both ships were the largest in the world.
- Both weighed 45 000 tons.
- Both had three propellers and two masts.

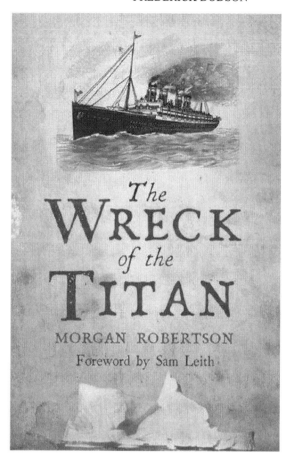

Even where the book is wrong, it is eerily close: The book says that the ship crashed into an iceberg 400 miles from Newfoundland at 25 knots. The real RMS Titanic crashed into an iceberg 400 miles from Newfoundland at 22.5. knots.

How is it possible that the book predicted something that would happen in 1912? There really are only two likely explanations: Either it was planned that way, or this is a case of Time Travel or Precognition (Precognition is also time travel). Maybe the author knew of the plans or the planners knew of the book. Or the author foresaw what would happen.

The Adventures of Baron Trump

This is a more recently discovered synchronicity. It relates to children's novels written in 1889 and 1893 by the lawyer Ingersoll Lockwood. The novels were not much of a success and remained obscure until 2017, when Donald Trump became President and synchronicity-hunters started noticing similarities between the books and what was playing out in real life.

The books are *"Travels and Adventures of Little Baron Trump"* and *"Baron Trumps Marvelous Underground Journey"*. The novel tells the story of German boy "Baron Trump" (Donald Trump does have German ancestry) "who discovers strange underground civilizations, offends the natives, flees from his entanglements with local women, and repeats this pattern until arriving back home at Castle Trump".

Some argue that this description is rather apt. Trumps supporters claim that he is fighting "weird underground civilizations" (as in "The Swamp"). His opponents claim that he "offends people" and "has extra-marital affairs". His Mar-a-Lago estate is in fact modelled after a Castle.

In the 19th Century, the novels were seen as a kind of response to or competition to Lewis Carroll's "Alice in Wonderland" books (1865), but they never achieved the same notoriety.

In 2017 people on the Internet and in the media began listing similarities between the book character and President Donald Trump and also the fact that his sons name is Barron Trump. Did Trump know of the books and give his son that name intentionally?

In 1900 Ingersoll Lockwood also published his dystopian book "The Last President" in which *New York City is riven by protests following the shock victory of a populist candidate in the 1896 presidential election*. Sound familiar?

I haven't read the books so I don't know whether there are further similarities or differences. But I find it curious that nobody noticed the books until Trump became President. They were then *retrospectively* discovered. I suggest that if we look more closely, we can find a prediction somewhere about any event in History. If you find that hard to believe, look no further than...

The Predictions of Jules Verne

Jules Verne was a poet, author and playwright who was born in 1828 and died in 1905, long before he could see his predictions come true. He wrote books that would today be assigned to the genre "Science Fiction", among them:

Five Weeks in a Balloon

From Earth to Moon

Journey to the Center of the Earth

Twenty Thousand Leagues under the Sea

Around the Moon

A Floating City

Around the World in Eighty Days

An Antarctic Mystery

And many, many more.

Jules Verne predicted that we'd one day have rockets, computers and airplanes. But even more odd is that Verne also predicted very specific objects. For instance, long before the Eiffel Tower was even conceived of, Verne described Paris as having a "skyline dominated by a large metallic tower". He said that Parisan life would be about Business and that women would become "Americanized" in that they fill their French language with American words. Instead of horses filling the streets, there would be metal vehicles (Verne wrote this long before the car was even thought of). Average people would sit in their offices and work at "computing machines" and "send paperwork to one another by facsimile machines".

Yes, Jules Verne uses the word "facsimile machine", which would, 100 years later, be shortened to "Fax Machine". His description of Paris is just a little too specific to be coincidental. As with the previous two examples on the wreck of the Titan and the Adventures of Baron Trump, we have to ask: Are we dealing with time travel, precognition or planning?

Image: Jules Verne, more of a time traveler than most psychics

Is there some ruling elite that secretly lays out their plans for the world, which Jules Verne got hold of or which he was assigned to write about? Or did Jules Verne travel to the future to glean what would be? While I have no doubt that ruling elites do a lot of planning, I believe that Jules Verne used *precognition,* just like many other science-fiction authors. I believe that some peoples consciousness is free and flexible and easily able to jump from time to time.

In his 1865 novel "From the Earth to the Moon" Jules Verne says there will be a manned flight to the Moon in the USA and that the rocket will take off from Florida with a splashdown in the Pacific. That's an exact prediction of the Apollo 11 mission, 100 years before it happened, long before anyone else even conceived of flying airplanes, not to mention rockets. In his novel he accurately predicts that the rocket will be made of aluminum, that passengers are protected from acceleration pressures by "shock absorbers" (addressing phenomena you'd normally only know in the age of high acceleration vehicles), and even details such as "retro-rockets", engines to decelerate rapidly. Apollo had such retro rockets so that they could slow down before landing on the moon.

Not only that, but Verne also said that Space was weightless. This is another fact that nobody was aware of in his time, because apparently nobody had travelled through space…yet.

Things get even more specific: The device used to launch the spacecraft in the novel was called Columbiad. In reality it was called Columbia. In his novel, the rocket makers consider a dozen sites for launching their rocket in Texas and Florida. In real life, NASA explored a dozen sites in Texas and Florida. The question arises: Did NASA use the name Columbia and the Florida location inspired by Jules Verne novels? Or was Verne simply a time traveler and a slight shift in timeline changed what he had foreseen from "Columbiad" to "Columbia"? Was rocketry itself inspired by Jules Verne? In that case, he created what he predicted. But, from researching countless synchronicities such as these, I'd say that NASA did not consciously choose these names and locations. They did not say "Let's make Jules Verne prediction come true". Rather, the press archives of the time, indicate that those in charge were completely unaware of the prediction, hoping to launch from Texas but then changing their plans due to political issues with Texas.

Another question that arises is whether the authors of these books help bring the things they predict, to life. They visualize it and then it exists in the field and finally it manifests. I'd say that's a real possibility, but it's not the main dynamic in play in these instances. Trumps presidency is more to do with what Trump visualized, than what Ingersoll Lockwood visualized. The Eiffel Tower is more the result of what its inventor visualized, than what Jules Verne predicted. I see these cases as more of a tapping into something that has a strong probability of coming true. What these authors are seeing are strong probabilities. Their consciousness is flexible enough to see.

The reason I believe so, is because I myself have predicted many things that have come true. In fact, I only predict things when I feel the strong probability. Otherwise I keep my mouth shut. I make a point of predicting various world events in the Live Seminars I do, just to demonstrate that one can sense strong probability.

It all makes one wonder: Who is this Jules Verne guy? Who is he really? But other science-fiction others have done similar. In fact, sci-fi authors have a *much better* track record of predicting the future than psychics and oracles. Many things that religious zealots, new agers and occultists have predicted has not come to pass and almost everything sci-fi authors have predicted has come to pass. It's not that psychic powers don't exits, it's that people have been looking in the wrong places.

Science Fiction has not only been the main source of interest in time travel, it has also taught a lot about society and human potential. It's my view that anything that can be imagined, is at some level already real or can be real. Imagination is a preview of the future or a peek into hidden realities. I have never believed in the idea that there is "reality" on the one side and "imagination" on the other. Imagination is filtering information from other realms.

The Predictions of H.G. Wells

Every technological reality of our times, began in Imagination. H.G. Wells predicted two World Wars, World Governments and flights to Mars. Jules Verne and H.G. Wells have both been called "the fathers of science fiction". Here's something he wrote in 1923 in his book "Men like Gods", a full 70 years before the invention of email:

"For in Utopia, except by previous arrangement, people do not talk together on the telephone," he writes. "A message is sent to the station of the district in which the recipient is known to be, and there it waits until he chooses to tap his accumulated messages. And any that one wishes to repeat can be repeated.

Then he talks back to the senders and dispatches any other messages he wishes. The transmission is wireless."

In his 1899 book "When the Sleeper Wakes" Wells said one day people will live in a Dystopian London where they will have things such as airplanes, television and audio books, but will suffer oppression and injustice.

In his even earlier book "The Island of Moreau" Wells discussed genetic engineering, surgical transplants and blood transfusions, things that were, back then, way above the heads of the general public.

In the 1898 book "Martians in the War of the Worlds", Wells speaks of Laser and Directed Energy Weapons, 60 years before any actually existed.

Even more strangely, Wells predicted that the Atom would be split and this would be used to harness extremely destructive powers. In his 1913 book "The World Set Free" he describes a devastating world war.

One of my favorite movies of childhood was "The Time Machine", made in 1959 and based on the novel by H.G. Wells. Seeing that H.G. Wells was interested in Time Travel, was he possibly a time traveler himself?

It was later publicly discovered that H.G. Wells was a British Intelligence Operative (MI6) and also, that his lover was a Russian spy. That adds some intrigue to his many predictions. Was he recruited by these secretive organizations because he knew so much, or did he knew so much because he was working for them? Probably some of both. Other notable authors include Aldous Huxley (Brave New World) and George Orwell (1984), who both predicted the mass surveillance society we live in today and Ray Bradbury, who predicted the moon landing, robots, virtual reality rooms, spy satellites, automated homes, cell phones, earbuds, wall TVs and large flat screen TVs and much more.

Not only have sci-fi authors written about time-travel, in a way they are themselves time-travelers. They stretch consciousness into the future and use their books to describe what they saw. Sci-Fi books are History books but the History they are describing is usually of some future timeline.

Non-Sci-Fi

Not all time travel comes from science-fiction authors. One of the most famous precognitions of all time comes from the author Edgar Allan Poe (1809-1849). His novel "The Narrative of Arthur Gordon Pym of Nantucket" was published in 1838 tells the story of a stowaway on a whaling vessel. There is an accident and four men survive the shipwreck and drift in an open boat at sea. Three of the men decide to murder one of them, so that the others can survive. The lower ranking cabin boy Richard Parker is killed and the others cannibalistically eat his remains to survive.

42 years later an almost identical incident occurred. In 1884 a Tom Dudley, and his three-man crew were sailing a vessel when they hit a storm, leaving them shipwrecked. The four

survived for 19 days without anything to eat until finally the captain chose to kill the weakest among them so that the others could survive. The survivors were found five days later and arrested for murder of the boy. The victims name had been Richard Parker, just like in Poe's novel.

An even more interesting case is that of the author Norman Mailer and his novel "Barbary Shore". The novel was not as popular as his others. It was about a character who would later be revealed to be a Russian spy.

After the books release, it was found out that an actual and real Russian spy had been arrested, living in the same house one room above Mailer. While Mailer had been writing the book, the reality of his fictional work was being played out right above his head! Mailer later said that the character came to him "spontaneously" and worked its way into the plot as the story progressed (that's to say, he didn't begin the book with that idea).

While this is not strictly a time travel story (even though it was somewhat predictive), it could be yet more evidence that we remote-view or remote sense what is going on around us and often work that into whatever we are doing.

In recent times, the cartoon shows "The Simpsons", "Family Guy" and "South Park" have been the most notorious for predicting real life events. You can look up the numerous predictions of these shows online. Many of them are so specific that it's surreal. So called "psychics" and "astrologers" are often criticized for being too general. We say that their "predictions" could be applied to anything. Not so for these cartoons.

Perhaps this has to do with the impersonal and non-local nature of paranormal abilities. When a self-proclaimed psychic intentionally attempts to see the future it is a different attitude than when a cartoonist allows his mind to wander freely and without expectation. I believe precognition works best, when the Ego is put aside and playfulness and desire to explore takes a front seat to trying to "prove something".

TIME TRAVEL

10

Claims of Time Travel

Every year there are thousands of claims of time travel from around the Globe. Most of these can easily be shown to be fake. Some of them are fake but are so well orchestrated, they are hard to detect as fraudulent. And then there are a few that might be genuine. It is useful to examine both fake and potentially genuine experiences to train the mind in discernment. There are stories that had me convinced, but later turned out to be fake. Some of these fraudulent stories were featured as "possibilities" in the first version of this book, that I wrote in 2002 and are removed in this version. But while browsing through the 2002-2003 book, looking to translate bits and pieces for this book, I did find one incredibly valuable gem. In 2002 I talked about having a dream about living in a distant country one day. And today I actually do live in exactly that distant country! I also say that I will live in a remote part of that distant country, and that's exactly where I live today. As I do not read my books after I write them, I had forgotten all about that little detail. Which means, personal proof for the reality of far-future prediction or time travel is contained within that original book!

What follows are a few claims of Time Travel from around the Internet in the last years.

Ancient Phones and Laptops

Quoted from Wikipedia:

In October 2010, Northern Irish filmmaker George Clarke uploaded a video clip entitled "Chaplin's Time Traveller" to YouTube. The clip analyzes bonus material in a DVD of the Charlie Chaplin film The Circus. Included in the DVD is footage from the film's Los Angeles premiere at Grauman's Chinese Theatre in 1928. At one point, a woman is seen walking by, holding up an object to her ear. Clarke said that, on closer examination, she was talking into a thin, black device that had appeared to be a "phone". Clarke concluded that the woman was possibly a time traveller. The clip received millions of hits and was the subject of televised news stories.

The photo above does not do the case justice. I recommend you look up the Video on the Internet yourself, typing "Charlie Chaplin's Time Machine".

Skeptics say the lady is likely wearing a hearing aid. But that wouldn't explain why she appears to be speaking into the device while walking around.

Nor is it the only such instance. Look up a Video about the "1938 Mobile Phone" or "1938 Cell Phone". It shows several women leaving a factory. One of them is speaking to someone on a handheld device that looks just like a cell phone. Again, the image below doesn't do it justice, watch the Video.

Skeptics have again proposed that the lady is wearing a "hearing aid", to which I again ask: Why would someone be talking into a hearing aid? She doesn't appear to be talking to the ladies around her.

Some people have come forward saying that the factory in the Video was Dupont and that this company had been secretly working on wireless telephones. They claimed the lady was testing a prototype of that wireless telephone. Which is true? I don't know. But surely, having a mobile phone invented in 1938 and kept secret is almost as extraordinary a claim as that of time travel.

On the other hand, if time travel exists, then it has always existed and we are bound to find a few anomalous objects throughout History.

The following two images from Ancient Greece, for example, have been going around the Internet as "ancient laptops":

The problem with these is that they could just as easily be make-up boxes or a number of other things. The handheld ear devices are less easy to explain, because people are seen talking while holding them to their ears.

Chronicles of the Future

Paul Dienach was a Swiss teacher who suffered from an illness that made him fall in and out of Comas. In 1921 he fell into a Coma for one year. After he woke up, he began writing a diary. He never published the diary. Before he passed away, he asked one of his students to keep the diary and keep it a secret. His writings are written from the perspective of another man, Andrew Northman, whose body and life he appears to have entered while in a Coma. Northman lived in the year 3906 AD. When he awakened in the future, people realized that Northman was gone. He wrote down everything he experienced, from the mindset-viewpoint of the 1920s. His story is available online for free or in a book titled "Chronicles of the Future". A quote from the book:

I stood at the entrance for a while, looking at the living room. A strangely large room with all kinds of bizarre - for me – things and those tall transparent doors that offered a panoramic view of the lush countryside, the slopes of the mountains and beyond. Then I started walking again but not for long. Every two steps I stopped and peered about. At some point, I turned around and saw the doctor looking at me with a curious expression on his face, - I'll never forget that look - but at that moment I didn't care about anything.

It was neither gold nor gems, like in fairy tales, that amazed me. Everything there was made of a beautiful type of crystal dressed in perfect combinations of pastel colors; sky blue, green, white and red. Everything, from the tables and chairs to the stools and the frames, gave you the impression of a colorless metal on which a soft light flowed incessantly in harmonic waves. Everything was bright and clear; even the flower pots and the crystal blooming springs of the flowers. However, if you came too close, like a curious child, believing you would find something in that transparent panorama of colors, the touch would rectify that first impression and the surfaces of the seats would prove soft and warm.

The doctor didn't rush me. Passing through the living room we found ourselves in a big hallway; that's where I finally saw people again after the isolation of the past days. It was a spacious vestibule that led right to the enormous main terrace. It was afternoon and the place was filled with light. Doctors and nurses were quietly chatting to each other standing up. At the sight of the chief doctor they discreetly stood aside and made way for us to pass. While walking past them I heard them whisper that name again, the name that everyone kept repeating all these days when in my presence: "Andrew Northam." I shivered. "Who is this Andrew Northam?" I wondered. The reality unfolds merciless before my eyes from all sides. There only remains for me to admit, along with the doctors, this unprecedented thing happening to me, which exceeds even the wildest dreams of the most overactive imagination.

I have read the entire story and my personal estimation is that it could easily be fiction, because it contains nothing specific enough to be of any tangible advantage. On the other hand, it is quite common that coma patients have paranormal experiences during their time "asleep". There is no shortage of experience reports of time travel from coma patients. So, there is the possibility that Paul Dienachs story is true. There is also the possibility that Dienach did have a brief time travel experience and then embellished and exaggerated the story with the idea of publishing a novel. The reason I doubt the story, as told by Dienachs student, is because it feels exaggerated. It is told, for example, that the story was kept strictly hidden by secret societies for a long time because they considered the information "too sacred" to be known by the public. But I couldn't find any part of the story that was "too sacred" and needed to be locked up. It sounded like many run-of-the-mill science-fiction stories I had read. I am always skeptical when people make claims of "mysterious secrets", "ancient secrets", "utmost secrecy" and such, as it feels and sounds more like a ploy for attention or a hyping of a product than a genuine piece of information.

Noah from the Future

On the Internet there are a few Videos by "Noah" a young guy or older teenager who claims to be from the future. In one Video he purports to be showing Video Footage on his phone from the year 2120. It shows shining skyscrapers and flying cars, as one might expect. Another video purports to show a chip implanted in his hand, which apparently allows for dematerialization of his body so that he can time travel. In another video he is supposedly shown doing a lie-detector test on his claims. In all of his Videos his face is blurred out because he claims to be afraid of being found by the Government and them assassinating him for "exposing the truth".

He says that his 'natural time' is the year 2030, the year his friends and family are in. He claims he was fired from his job during a mission in the year 2017 and is now stuck in the year 2019.

I take his story as an example of *thousands of similar claims on the Internet*. These are fun to watch and it's good to ask "What if?". But it's also be healthy to ask "What if not?" The problem is that no hard proof is provided for Noahs claims. None, whatsoever. Nor does he make any predictions that aren't easy to predict by anyone. Every researcher and time traveler should take this to heart: iI you want to know whether something is authentic or not, check what the bottom-line benefit is or whether you have learned anything new. Many of these time travelers have less predictive powers than your average every day joe, than me or than sci-fi authors.

As already hinted at, genuine time travelers do not feel the need to prove it to the public. Their time travel is an experience of personal exploration. Perhaps they wish to share some of their experiences with others. In that case, they might write a useful book. They will hardly just put up a sensationalistic video on the Internet of little value. There are real time travelers. But many of them won't tell you so.

11

Dimensional Doorways

Our fantasy and sci-fi tales are full of Dimensional Doorways, Portals and Stargates. They are also found in ancient fairy tales, folk tales and legends. Yes, I believe all fiction is based on reality and that there are portals connecting distant locations on earth, distant locations between planets, locations between galaxies even, connect different locations in time and between parallel universes. The behavior of dimensional doorways in old folk tales is similar to that of wormholes. They apply the de-materialization method.

Ancient Stargates

Puerta de Hayu Marca, Peru

This structure was re-discovered in 1996, by travel tour guide Jose Luis Delgado Mamani. He had been dreaming about a marble gateway with a smaller inset door from which a mysterious blue light emanated and which led to a shimmering tunnel. When he discovered this structure he almost fainted, in recognition of what he had dreamed. He called it "Gate of the Gods", based the legends of the natives around Lake Titicaca, who claimed there were Gates the Gods used to travel to distant places and that this was one of them.

If you look closely, you can see the doorway is a near-T-shape or a small and a large doorway. The large one is seven meters (22 feet) wide and high. The small doorway is two meters (6.5 ft) high. Representatives of the natives are said to claim that the large door is for the "Gods" and the small door for heroic mortals who dare enter the land of the Gods to become immortal themselves.

According to legend, when Peru was invaded in the 16th Century, Incan priest Amuru Maru fled with a golden disk called "The Key of the Gods of the Seven Rays". He found the portal that was guarded by Shaman priests. He presented the disk. The priests performed a ritual, the doorway opened and Amuru Maru stepped into a shining blue light.

Whether there is any truth whatsoever to these legends, I don't know. I'd assume that a gate such as this one can only be opened with the right code or movements. I note that almost all legends that I have read on Dimensional Doorways, say that the light of the portal is blue or blue and white.

Mher's Door, Turkey

Quoted from Internet Sources:

"Mher's Door" is a sacred cave near the Van fortress. According to Armenian traditions, Little Mher, who is the last hero of national epic "Daredevils of Sassoon", closed himself inside the cave because he was outraged at the world's injustices. According to saga, once a year, on the festival of Roses or in the night of destinies, when heaven and earth kiss each other, Mher with his fiery horse comes out, walks in heaven and on earth, but convinced that the earth cannot stand his weight, goes back to his place. It is said that In the future, Mher will come out of the cave, will release the "World of Armenians" from evil forces and will create a happy kingdom. In the legend the idea of freeing the world from the power of evil spirits and the second coming of the God Mithra are still preserved.

I am citing this is one of hundreds of examples of saying these doors are portals to other realms. The doors are common across every culture and region.

Tiahuanaco, Bolivia, 'Gate of the Sun'

This is yet another portal referred to as a doorway to the "land of the gods". Apparently sun-god Viracocha appeared at this location and decided to create humanity from here. The structure is estimated to be 14 000 years old. The gateway displays human beings with what look like rectangular helmets. The Sun God is above the arch, with rays of light around his head.

Ranmasu Uyana Stargate, Sri Lanka

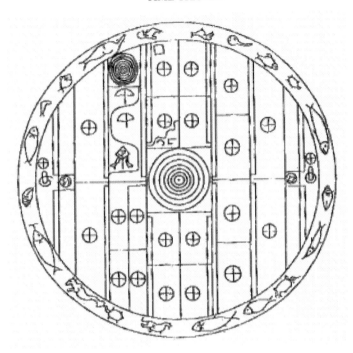

The drawing above is a carving on a massive piece of stone wall, near a gate-like structure. It is claimed to be a star map and that the symbols on the rock are the code that opens the gate to the stars for travel from this world to other areas of the Universe. Opposite the carving are what appear to be four stone chairs. The name of the star map is Sakwala Chakraya, which translates as "the rotating circle of the Universe".

I present this as an example of portals that involve rotation or spinning. There are many more, especially in South America and Native America.

There are many other Dimensional Doorway examples I could cite here, such as the Bermuda Triangle, Abu Ghurab, Abydos, Stonehenge and Gobekli Tepe, but these should suffice as good examples of such claims. Lacking any knowledge to know whether these can be activated, there is no point in dwelling on them.

Scientists attempting to open portal to a parallel universe

Quoted from a newspaper article published here:

https://www.independent.co.uk/news/science/parallel-universe-portal-mirror-world-science-stranger-things-oak-ridge-a8987681.html

Could 2019 be the year humans open the first portal to a shadowy dimension which mirrors our own world?

Scientists in Oak Ridge National Laboratory in eastern Tennessee hope so, and have completed building equipment they are to test this summer which may allow us the first glimpse of a parallel universe which could be identical in many ways to our own, with mirror particles, mirror planets and possibly even mirror life.

That is according to Leah Broussard, the physicist behind the project, who described the attempt to reveal a hidden shadow world as "pretty wacky" in an interview with NBC last week.

The discovery of a concealed mirror world may sound like science fiction from the Stranger Things series, but it has been repeatedly suggested by physicists as a tempting means of explaining anomalous results. However, as yet, hard evidence such a realm exists has refused to manifest itself.

One set of anomalous results, and the ones which inspired the research, date back to the 1990s, when particle physicists were measuring the time it took for neutron particles to break down into protons once they were removed from an atom's nucleus.

Two separate experiments saw the neutrons broke down at differing rates, instead of decaying and becoming protons at exactly the same rate, as was expected.

In one, the free neutrons were captured by magnetic fields and herded into laboratory bottle traps, and in the other they were detected by the subsequent appearance of proton particles from a nuclear reactor stream.

Those particles fired out in the stream from the nuclear reactor lived on average for 14 minutes and 48 seconds – nine seconds longer than those from the bottle traps.

It may sound like a small difference, but it has troubled scientists.

But the existence of a mirror world offers a credible explanation: That there are two separate neutron lifetimes, and it could be that around 1 per cent of neutrons could be crossing the divide between our reality and the mirror world before crossing back and then emitting a detectable proton.

The new experiment will fire a beam of neutrons at an impenetrable wall. On the other side of the wall, a neutron detector will be set up, which normally would expect to detect nothing.

But if the detector does register the presence of neutrons, the theory is that they may have gone through the wall by "oscillating" into the mirror world – becoming mirror neutrons – and reappearing in this universe, and more specifically the lab in Tennessee.

"Only the ones that can oscillate and then come back into our universe can be detected," Ms Broussard told the New Scientist in June.

Furthermore, the team will set up magnetic fields on either side of the wall, which they can alter in strength. It is hoped certain strengths may assist the oscillation of the particles.

Despite the tidy theory, the team is playing down the chances of revealing reality's shadowy twin.

"I fully expect to measure zero," Ms Broussard said of the initial tests.

But if they do detect a neutron on the far side of the wall, it could have profound implications.

"If you discover something new like that, the game totally changes," Ms Broussard told NBC.

The existence of a mirror world could also explain our universe's lack of the isotope Lithium 7, which physicists believe doesn't match the quantities the Big Bang would have created.

The detection of high-energy cosmic rays which come from beyond our galaxy could also be explained by the existence of the mirror world.

They are too powerful to have travelled only through the observed universe, but if they had oscillated into the mirror realm and then back out again, it could explain why that is the case.

Parallel Universes of Earth

Just like there are many versions of you, there are many versions of Planet Earth on different parallel timelines that exist simultaneously. Are these parallel worlds elsewhere or else-when? Neither. Elsewhere might be other Planets. Else-when might be other times on this Planet or in this Universe. Parallel Universes seem to take place on another dimensional axis.

There are versions of Earth that are similar to ours, they mirror our world. And there are versions that are so different, they wouldn't even be recognized as Planet Earth. Below, I am featuring some of the more well-known. Some of these are known through our "fairy tales" and "science fiction stories". If certain versions of Earth keep coming to various authors of different times, across many cultures, that's because all of these authors are perceiving a world that really exists. Some of these worlds I am aware of personally. The number of possible worlds seems to be unlimited.

The purpose of presenting these two you, are to shift your awareness away from the known and to make your thinking more flexible. Before finding Dimensional Doorways, you'll want to have examples of places they might lead to.

FREDERICK DODSON

Empty Planet Earth

There appear to be thousands of Earths that are uninhabited, including a version that looks just like our Earth, but without people. Some of them were once inhabited and are not anymore. Others are deserted as if by nuclear disaster. Some have a few people on them, perhaps because they found doors to this parallel universe or because they were left behind there by their spacefaring civilizations or for other mysterious reasons.

As a child I sometimes visited an empty version of Earth in night dreams. In one of them, all buildings were standing but there were no people, as if there was a bomb that got rid of only the people and left the buildings standing. I saw the same Earth in a future version, a few hundred years from now. And finally, I've also seen ancient empty Earths full of dense rain forest and dinosaur-like creatures. What does all that mean? I don't know. I do know it's incredibly interesting to visit and explore these places. Earth without humans has a strange feel to it. You might think that that must be much better, but it's not. Humans are what bring life, love and spirit to the Planet. Without it, it's just a vast, wild terrain.

Historically Changed Earth

The most fascinating versions of Earth are those that took another turn in History than we did. There is, for example, a version of our Planet in which the Egyptian Kingdom is still blossoming. It never ended. They are a spacefaring civilization, ruled from Egypt. There's a world in which Nazi Germany won the war. What is Europe and Russia to us, is the "Deutsches Reich". It's opponents are America and Asia. All of Europe is build according to the grandiose, megalomaniac visions of Hitlers architect Albert Speer. There's a TV Show, "The Man in the High Castle", based on Phillip K. Dicks science-fiction novel that portrays this parallel world. There is a version of the world that is primarily ruled by the Chinese. Any variation you can imagine, exists. Your Imagination can give you access to the most probable ones immediately. Remember a large historic event and imagine, it took a different turn. Follow the progression of events.

Magical Planet Earth

This is a series of very specific parallel universes that portray a mix of medieval states, fairy tale scenarios and magic. Our fantasy books and movies are based on these worlds. Lord of the Rings, Harry Potter, etc. are a reality here. You might see flying dragons, people carrying magic wands, witches turning into frogs, etc. These are planets without much logic or order. And as exciting as that might sound, I've found that they are a bit more dark, dense and gothic than our version of Earth.

Planet of Games

This is also a specific type of parallel earth in which life is celebrated as a game. These people have developed every game and variation imaginable. There are, of course, positive

FREDERICK DODSON

and less positive versions of this world. In the darkest versions of the Games Worlds, human life means nothing. Gigantic Amusement Arenas showcase gladiator-like fights and take pleasure in seeing people suffer, bleed and die. The more violence, the more entertaining it is for these people. I've also seen a sadistic game in which a type of squash is played, but the balls contain a kind of acid that kills those who come in touch with it. The game is played with only one living survivor at the end, after hundreds of people have painfully died. More positive variations of this world have cultivated sports and games as a substitute for war. Nobody dies in these games. If there is a conflict between two nations, it is carried out in games. I saw, for example, an air-force game which the people prepare for many months. Once it starts, the whole world is watching. Airplanes that are hit, are removed from the game. The pilot doesn't die but is catapulted out of his plane and lands by parachute. It appears to me that the 1983 movie "Tron"(and the 2010 remake) is based on ideas taken from the Games Planet, as I've seen similar there.

Glowing Earth

This parallel world version is taking place on a higher frequency. It's the spiritual utopia so many of us dream of. Perhaps we are moving toward something similar. Technology and Ecology harmonize on this planet. All the technology is extremely advanced, silent and clean. Population density is low. You have several beautiful small cities with round, glass-like or crystal buildings, at around 10 000 people per city. Expansion of consciousness is one of the primary interests of the people, hence these people know and consciously travel other worlds. They find joy in helping.

Dark Earth

The opposite polarity to the glowing Earth also exists, of course. It's the place of nightmares. From our perspective, it is ruled by the mentally ill. One of their practices is to genetically interbreed various animals or even cross animals with humans. The climate reflects the people's mentality in that it's usually cloud covered across the whole planet and much darker than our version. The amount of suffering is enormous, but I wont dwell on it here.

And that's only a few versions of Earth. Of course, there are also parallel versions of other planets and galaxies. In other words, there is no limit to thing that could be discovered. No matter what you can imagine, somewhere out there, there is a whole world on it. One of the greatest lies humanity tells itself is that there is only this world, or even only the physical world. But even the religious are limited. In the Abrahamic religions there is only Heaven and Earth. In Buddhism there is only Reincarnation to the same Planet. But the truth is, that the Multi-Verse is vaster and grander than any of those ideas.

What's the purpose of all of these worlds? Why were they created? They were created for our immortal souls to experience. Sometimes we get so lost in exploring all of these worlds, like in a maze, that we forget where home is, where source is. It's important to know that all these paranormal abilities, trips to different planets, time travels, parallel universe travels are not the same thing as "going home", as spiritual ascension.

Let's say there are 10 levels of frequency or consciousness. In relation to that scale, we are currently at level three consciousness. The next level of humanity is 4. There are very few individuals residing at level four. Some, who have gained a glimpse of level four, are ignorantly called "Enlightened". The next level is like having a wider view and more amazing experiences. Level 4 contains all levels below it, but not any above it. To get an understanding of the difference between things, take a pencil and a piece of paper and draw as follows:

1. Draw eight concentric circles
2. Planet Earth: Draw a small dot within the inner third circle
3. Solar System: Circle the small dot with a small circle.
4. Interplanetary travel: Draw a small line from the small dot, through the small circle outwards.
5. Ascend a level of consciousness: Draw a line from the dot to the fourth circle
6. Parallel Universes: Put the pencil somewhere on the Paper and lift it half an inch into the air. That's the location of your parallel universe. Lift it another inch up in the air. That's your next parallel universe. Hold

it 5 inches in the air. Now that's a parallel universe that is very dissimilar to your home universe. You could stack several papers above the first one and each would be a parallel universe. These papers however, are two dimensional. In reality, the universe is three dimensional. If all this where three dimensional, where is the parallel world? You'd need to view from a fourth or fifth dimension to see it.

7. Time Travel: Put your pencil just a millimeter above the dot that symbolizes Earth.

8. Imagine now the 8 circles are actually stairs that rise from inside to the outer circles. If you can imagine that, then you will notice the 4th, 5th, 6th, 7th and 8th levels of consciousness are high enough to "naturally" contain a few parallel universes. The parallel worlds bordering level 3 are easier to explore from level 4 because they are contained in it.

These are, of course, insufficient illustrations, but they help the mind to grasp that there are differences.

The funny thing is, people have barely even explored their own Universe, not to mention trillions of other universes. There's certainly no lack of things to do. The first thing you might want to do in the afterlife, is visit a good travel agency.

A Sense of Vibration

A sense of vibration is a talent some people are born with and also a skill that can be learned. It's knowing which category, reality or corresponding field an event, emotion, place, time, person, fashion, thing, philosophy, ideology, attitude belongs to. It's the ability to sense different levels of consciousness. A sense of vibration can also sense the difference between an object that is, say 50 000 B.C. and one that is 15 000 B.C. or the difference between a cityscape of the year 2200 AD vs 2500 vs 4000.

If you have a good sense of vibration, then you know that some of what we are currently predicting about our future is accurate but a lot of it is also inaccurate. But you don't bother telling people, because many of them get angry when their cherished beliefs are contradicted. With a good sense of vibration you are often at odds with what most other people "are saying".

Back when I wrote my first time travel book in 2001, was telling people that nothing will come of "the year 2012" or any "Mayan Prophecy". I told them there would be no "technological singularity" in the next 20 years, no widespread "climate disaster" and also no "Armageddon". There will be no "overpopulation crisis", no "demographic crisis" and no "World War III". I also said there will be not be much interstellar travel in the next twenty years. And people who believed one or several of these things would get upset with me, but I was correct about every one of these things. Today, I largely keep quiet because I don't wish to waste my time with all kinds of messages requesting "clarification" from upset people. If one is upset that their beliefs are contradicted, then these beliefs are usually not chosen freely, from an intuitive, vibratory sense of reality. They are, indoctrinated or conditioned through repetition in mass media. That said, I will share a few good things that will happen in the next 10 years, as a Testimony to the ability to sense forward in time.

The 2020s (2020 to 2029) will be surprisingly peaceful. There will be no major World War. Most wars fought out will be "silent" or outside of public awareness. There will be some regional conflicts, as there are already. Cures for AIDS, Cancer and other ailments will become available. New, durable materials will be invented or discovered. Poverty and Illiteracy rates will continue to drop like they have been for the last decades. Consciousness Research, Spirituality and Self-Improvement will continue to gain in popularity as it has been. Many of the Corporate Monopolies, as they exist today, will start falling apart. Most people predict we will become more global, but actually the opposite is true: People will become more local. Government will become more local. Journalism will become more local and driven by local citizens. The reason is that mass-attention has been global to the extreme in the last 20 years, with the rise of the Internet. Because consciousness follows pendulum movements, it will go to the other side, to localism. Flying Cars will be slow in coming, first there will be more electric cars. New forms of generating and storing energy will be discovered. The existence of extraterrestrial Beings will be obvious to most within the next ten years. These probabilities are easy to see based on current energy and mass-intention.

This completes the book "Time Travel". I have recorded accompanying guided Audio Meditations with some of the Time Travel Techniques in this book. You can find them in the "Members section" of my website

www.realitycreation.org